$7.95

DINING IN—KANSAS CITY

Boots Mathews and James Rieger

Foreword by Henry Bloch

PEANUT BUTTER PUBLISHING
Peanut Butter Towers · Seattle, Washington 98134

OTHER TITLES IN SERIES:

Feasting In—Atlanta
Dining In—Baltimore
Dining In—Boston
Dining In—Chicago
Dining In—Dallas
Dining In—Honolulu/Maui
Dining In—Houston (Vols. I & II)
Dining In—Los Angeles
Dining In—Minneapolis/
            St. Paul
Dining In—Monterey
            Peninsula
Dining In—New Orleans
Dining In—Pittsburgh
Dining In—Portland
Dining In—St. Louis
Dining In—San Francisco
Dining In—Seattle (Vol. II)
Dining In—Toronto

Copyright © 1980 by Peanut Butter Publishing.
All rights reserved.
Printed in the United States of America.
ISBN 0-89716-041-X

Second Printing January, 1981.

CONTENTS

Foreword   *v*
Acknowledgment   *vi*
Preface   *vii*
Alameda Plaza Roof   1
Al-Roubaie Restaurant   13
American Restaurant   21
La Bonne Auberge   29
Bristol Bar & Grill   39
Costello's Greenhouse   47
The Dinner Horn   55
Harry Starker's   67
Houlihan's Old Place   77
Italian Gardens   87
Jasper's   97
Jennie's   105
La Méditérranée   111
Nabil's   119
Plaza III   127
Princess Garden   137
The Prospect   145
Savoy Grill   155
Stephenson's Old Apple Farm   163
Stroud's   171
Tasso's   179
Index   *185*

FOREWORD

Over the years, as founder and President of H & R Block, I have found it necessary to travel from my home city to many other parts of the country and world. Obviously, on a number of occasions I have had the opportunity to dine in many places, both simple and elaborate. The offerings and cuisine have varied in style and sophistication and I have found all of the meals interesting. Yet there is something very special about the pleasure I find dining in Kansas City—and, to my way of thinking, nothing else compares to the best we offer here.

It is a very taxing problem to select the one best place or meal that will offer just what is wanted or needed. The problem is made more complicated when entertaining an out-of-town visitor is the reason for dining out. How can one find that part of the Kansas City dining experience that best typifies what the city has to offer?

Kansas City does offer a veritable cornucopia of dining opportunities. Our steaks and our barbeque specialties are world famous. Less well known are such delights as our fried chicken. And, restaurants that feature ethnic specialties, haute cuisine and assorted other fine foods continue to prosper here.

Dining In—Kansas City offers a novel solution to a chronic problem. With it, one can choose the finest of dining out while staying in. The discriminating host or hostess can present a meal for friends, guests or family that is based on a selection of the best of the favorites.

In addition, this book allows us to more finely appreciate the care and skill involved in the preparation of a favorite dish while dining out. Regardless, **Dining In—Kansas City** is a valuable collection of information and recipes that any Kansas City host or hostess should be pleased to own.

Here, then, is **Dining In—Kansas City**. Use it to select your favorite dining experiences out—or in. You will find it very enjoyable.

Henry W. Bloch

ACKNOWLEDGMENT

Our special thanks to Joel Laner

BLM and JLR

PREFACE

In recent years there has been a restaurant population explosion in Kansas City. No longer is the choice limited to a few steak houses. One can find almost every nationality and style of dining represented. The choice of atmosphere and décor ranges from elegant to country, conservative to the latest trend.

New young chefs have brought an interest in nutritional cooking: vegetables are steamed . . . colors remain bright. French chefs are adding nouvelle cuisine to their traditional menus. Ethnic groups have contributed new spices and taste combinations. Demographic specialists have introduced the concept of food and décor themes. Historic restoration and civic pride have opened up new-old neighborhoods that have inspired imaginative décor and menus.

The reader will find a sampling of this variety in these pages. The menus and recipes range from simple "down home" cooking to complex French recipes. If you can read, you can cook. Select your mood for the evening . . . French, Pennsylvania Dutch, Mediterranean, simple country . . . and have fun "Goin' to Kansas City."

Boots Mathews

alameda plaza

Dinner for Four

Chilled Potage Singapore

Lobster Américaine

Straw Potatoes

Lemon Sherbet with Kiwi

Saltimbocca alla Roma

Artichoke Florentine

Bibb Lettuce and Spinach Salad

Camembert Beignets

Chocolate Mousse Raphael

Wines:
With Lobster—Dry Creek Fumé Blanc, 1978
With Saltimbocca—Spring Mountain Cabernet
Sauvignon, Les Trois Cuvées
With Beignets and Mousse—Dow's Board Room Port

Max Hensel, Vice-President of Food and Beverages
John Lombardo, Food and Beverage Manager
Jess Barbosa, Executive Chef

The Alameda Plaza Roof Restaurant is atop the Alameda Plaza Hotel. The hotel, which opened in 1972, has in a few short years acquired an international reputation as one of America's outstanding luxury hotels. One gets a spectacular view of Kansas City's Country Club Plaza on the way up to the restaurant via the hotel's all-glass exterior elevator.

The Spanish/Moorish architecture and décor of the Country Club Plaza pervades the mood of the Alameda Plaza Roof Restaurant. Dark, heavy beams, high ceilings and wrought-iron decorative accessories complement the architecture. The predominant colors are warm oranges and reds with burnt-orange tablecloths. There is a formal air to the dining room, but it is not stiff. Windows along the north and south sides of the dining room give a beautiful view of the Country Club Plaza night or day. The seating ranges from comfortable, intimate booths, to small tables for two or more, on up to large round tables for parties of ten.

The food is the result of a congenial team of two: John Lombardo, Food and Beverage Manager, and Jess Barbosa, Executive Chef. John Lombardo started as a dishwasher and busboy at the age of fourteen. Since that early beginning, he has trained in every area from baking to tableside cooking. John plans to offer more tableside cooking at the restaurant. Chef Barbosa got his culinary start courtesy of the United States Navy. He has come a long way since those days. At the Alameda he is running a large commercial kitchen but with the personal attention and pride of the master chef. Not a detail escapes his eye. Jess and John both emphasize the importance of top-quality ingredients to get good results.

The Alameda Plaza Roof Restaurant has been awarded the Ivy Award by *Institutions* and the Silver Spoon Award by *Outlook*. The restaurant offers a table d'hôte menu each night in addition to a wide range of menu items at lunch and dinner.

Wornall Road at Ward Parkway

CHILLED POTAGE SINGAPORE

This recipe makes 3 cups.

9 ounces cream cheese, room temperature
2 cups canned, undiluted beef consommé
Pinch of garlic powder
2 teaspoons curry powder
Light cream as needed
8 sprigs fresh watercress

1. Place cream cheese in blender and slowly blend in 1 cup consommé. Mix well.
2. Add remaining 1 cup beef consommé, garlic powder and curry powder. Mix for 1 minute.
3. Chill overnight or at least 2 to 3 hours in a plastic container. The mixture should thicken to the consistency of yogurt.
4. Just before serving, thin with cream to the texture of a potage or cream soup. Serve in a champagne saucer, margarita glass or silver supreme. Garnish with 2 sprigs of fresh watercress.

Note: This has very simple ingredients, but ends up tasting quite exotic. The important technique in this recipe is to add the consommé very gradually to the softened cream cheese.

LOBSTER AMERICAINE

½ teaspoon saffron
1 bay leaf, crumbled
1 cup dry white wine
¼ pound butter
¼ cup finely chopped carrots
¼ cup finely chopped celery
¼ cup finely chopped onions
¼ cup finely chopped shallots or scallions
2 large tomatoes, peeled, seeded and finely chopped (about 3 cups)
6 tablespoons tomato juice
½ teaspoon lemon juice
2 tablespoons finely chopped fresh parsley
Salt and pepper
4 (4-ounce) lobster tails (fresh or frozen)
1 cup milk
2 eggs
1 cup flour
1 tablespoon Parmesan cheese

1. Soak the saffron and bay leaf in wine and set aside.
2. In a heavy saucepan or skillet, melt 4 tablespoons of butter over moderate heat. When the foam subsides, stir in the carrots and celery. Cook about 5 minutes.
3. Add onions, shallots, tomatoes, tomato juice and lemon juice. Continue cooking another 3 minutes. Add parsley and the white wine with saffron and bay leaf. Cook for 2 minutes. Season to taste with salt and pepper. Set sauce aside.
4. Split lobster tails in half lengthwise. Pull meat out.
5. Beat milk and eggs together. Combine flour, salt, pepper and Parmesan. Dip lobster tails in milk-egg mixture, then dredge in Parmesan flour and shake off excess.
6. Melt remaining butter in a skillet and sauté the lobster tails on one side for 3 to 4 minutes. Turn and repeat on the other side until golden brown and cooked through.

7. Pour sauce over sautéed lobster tails and allow to cook on low heat for a few minutes more.
8. Serve in small oval ramekins with **Straw Potatoes.**

Note: Jess Barbosa recommends using African rock lobster for the best results. The meat of African lobsters is firmer than that of lobsters grown in other areas. You can use drained, canned tomatoes in place of fresh, but fresh are better. Tomato juice will add both color and flavor to the sauce.

Lobster Américaine is in the spirit of nouvelle cuisine. The sauce contains only vegetables, wine and seasonings—no cream or flour. The vegetables are cooked lightly so they remain crisp and make a nice textural contrast with the lobster.

Straw Potatoes
Pommes Pailles

3 medium potatoes
Fresh lemon juice
Vegetable oil as needed
Salt to taste

1. Peel potatoes and shape into long rectangles. Place in cold water with a little fresh lemon to prevent discoloration.
2. Cut the potatoes into julienne strips (about $1/16$"). Rinse cut potatoes in cold water and wrap in a dampened towel.
3. Heat oil to a depth of at least 3" in a heavy pan or fryer until temperature is 330°.
4. Pat the potato strips dry with a paper towel and drop into the hot oil a handful at a time. (If a frying basket is not available to lower the potatoes into the oil, use a skimmer or slotted spoon to lift them out.) Turn the potatoes constantly until pale brown on all sides. Hold on paper towels.
5. Just prior to serving, fry the potatoes quickly at 360° for 2 to 3 minutes until golden brown on all sides. Drain, salt and serve immediately.

LEMON SHERBET WITH KIWI

This is to cleanse and refresh the palate. Another name for this type of sherbet is spoom.

Per serving:

Sugar
Fresh lime
1 small scoop lemon sherbet
½ kiwi fruit, skinned
Dash Guyot's Crème de Cassis
1 sprig fresh mint (candied violet may be
    substituted.

1. Rim a 5- to 6-ounce champagne saucer in sugar, wetting the edges first with a lime.
2. Scoop the lemon sherbet into the glass.
3. Cut the kiwi into slices then cut each slice in half. Arrange a border around the sherbet.
4. Dot the sherbet with crème de cassis and garnish with fresh mint sprig. (Indent the top of the sherbet with the bowl of a demitasse spoon to retain some of the liqueur and add to the attraction.)

SALTIMBOCCA ALLA ROMA

8 (2-ounce) veal cutlets, pounded flat
¼ pound butter
8 (1-ounce) slices prosciutto ham
1 cup all-purpose flour
Salt and pepper
2 eggs, slightly beaten
1 tablespoon olive oil
1 teaspoon fresh minced shallots
½ cup fresh or canned beef or veal stock
½ cup Chablis
1 cup fresh sliced mushrooms

1. Sauté veal very lightly on both sides in 2 tablespoons butter.
2. Lay veal cutlets flat and cover each with a slice of prosciutto. Press pairs of cutlets together, sandwiching 2 slices ham between each 2 cutlets.
3. Season the flour with salt and pepper. Dip the meat sandwiches in the lightly beaten eggs, then in the seasoned flour and shake off excess flour.
4. Melt 2 tablespoons butter with olive oil and sauté the meat sandwiches over medium heat until brown. Remove to a warm platter.
5. Remove most of the fat from the skillet, leaving only a thin film. Add shallots and heat for 1 minute, stirring.
6. Add stock and wine and reduce by boiling for 2 to 4 minutes. Remove any brown fragments from the bottom or sides of the pan. When the sauce has reduced to a soupy glaze, adjust seasoning with salt and pepper.
7. Remove pan from heat and stir 1½ to 2 tablespoons of soft butter into sauce to thicken. Set aside and keep warm.
8. Sauté sliced mushrooms in remaining butter and salt and pepper to taste.
9. Pour sauce over veal and serve with sautéed mushrooms

ARTICHOKE FLORENTINE

4 cups frozen leaf spinach, defrosted and well drained
2 tablespoons minced onion
1 tablespoon lemon juice
4 tablespoons melted butter
Salt and pepper to taste
Nutmeg to taste
2 large artichokes
Pinch of salt
1 bay leaf
2 tablespoons vegetable oil
Juice from ½ lemon
1 hard-cooked egg

1. Chop spinach very fine in a commercial chopper or blender. Combine with onion in a mixing bowl.
2. Add lemon juice, 3 tablespoons butter, salt, pepper and nutmeg to mixture. Adjust seasoning if necessary.
3. Place artichokes in a pan and cover with cold water. Add salt, bay leaf, oil and lemon juice. (The lemon juice flavors the artichokes and helps preserve the color.) Bring water to a slow boil and cook 20 to 40 minutes or until leaves pull out easily. Remove artichokes from water and plunge into cold water to cool quickly and preserve the color.
4. Preheat oven to 350°.
5. Split artichokes from top to bottom into 2 sections and remove the choke (purple, hairy area) with a spoon or your fingers.
6. Fill each half with the spinach mixture and bake in preheated oven approximately 20 minutes. Baste with remaining melted butter after 10 minutes.
7. Garnish with a slice of hard-cooked egg.

BIBB LETTUCE AND SPINACH SALAD

6 ounces fresh spinach, washed and stems removed
2 heads Bibb or Kentucky limestone lettuce, broken in pieces
4 slices fresh bacon, cooked and crumbled
2 hard-cooked eggs, chopped
3 ounces fresh bean sprouts
12 cherry tomatoes
Creamy Anchovy Dressing

Combine spinach and lettuce and portion onto chilled glass plates. Garnish attractively with remaining ingredients. Serve with **Creamy Anchovy Dressing.**

Creamy Anchovy Dressing

This recipe makes 4 cups.

1½ cups salad oil
½ cup cider vinegar
1 teaspoon garlic powder
½ teaspoon dry English mustard
Salt and white pepper to taste
Oregano to taste
Garlic powder to taste
Chopped parsley to taste
2 eggs
2 teaspoons anchovy paste

In a bowl, combine all ingredients except eggs and anchovy paste. Beat the eggs and anchovy paste together and then beat into the mixture until smooth.

This dressing has a bitey taste. It could be used on a variety of greens.

CAMEMBERT BEIGNETS

This recipe makes 15 to 20 walnut-size beignets.

6 ounces Camembert or Brie cheese, room temperature, crust trimmed
½ cup plus 2 tablespoons freshly grated Parmesan cheese
½ cup water
¼ pound butter
1 cup all-purpose flour
2 eggs, slightly beaten, room temperature

1. Place the cheese in a baine-marie (double boiler) to melt slowly. Cheese gets stringy if it is put over direct heat.
2. Heat water and butter together until butter is melted.
3. Whisk flour into melted butter and water and cook about 3 minutes, stirring constantly. (Jess Barbosa prefers a wooden spoon to a whisk for this operation.) Remove from heat and cool 2 minutes.
4. Beat eggs into mixture slowly. Add cheeses.
5. Heat 2" to 3" oil to 325°.
6. Shape teaspoons of mixture into mini-football shapes. Drop into oil and cook until golden brown. The beignets will float to the top of the oil when they are done.
7. Drain on paper towels and serve immediately.

Note: Beignets can be prepared to this point ahead of time and then can be re-warmed in the oven for 10 minutes at 325°. To give a little more zing to the beignets, add a touch of cayenne.

Beignets are the French equivalent of fritters. They may be served as an accompaniment to dessert, soup or salad.

CHOCOLATE MOUSSE RAPHAEL

This is a rich but very light chocolate mousse. It is such a favorite at the Raphael Hotel, the Alameda's sister across the street, that it is served nightly there.

This recipe makes approximately 6 servings.

2 ounces bitter chocolate
2 tablespoons cocoa
¾ cup powdered sugar
3 tablespoons coffee
3 tablespoons Kahlua
3 tablespoons dark crème de cacao
3 tablespoons Grand Marnier
2 egg yolks, slightly beaten
2 cups heavy cream
5 egg whites
Unsweetened whipped cream (optional)

1. In a double boiler, melt chocolate and cocoa together. Stir until cocoa is blended and smooth.
2. Add powdered sugar and half of the coffee, stirring until well blended.
3. Add Kahlua, crème de cacao, Grand Marnier and remaining coffee. Stir until smooth and free of lumps.
4. Remove from heat and allow to cool. Add slightly beaten egg yolks.
5. Whip heavy cream, add to base and mix well.
6. Beat egg whites to stiff peaks and fold into cream and base mixture.
7. Chill for 1 to 2 hours. Serve with a spoonful of unsweetened whipped cream, if desired.

Al-Roubaie

Dinner for Four

Homos

Al-Roubaie Soup

Turkish Lamb Kabob

Potatoes Al-Roubaie

Strawberries Romanoff

Wines:

With Homos—a Chablis
With Lamb—a Médoc

Kassim Al-Roubaie, Owner
Mohammed Hamid, Chef

While some say "The world is my oyster," Kassim Al-Roubaie, the proprietor of Al-Roubaie Restaurant, would say the Mediterranean is his oyster. For his menu, he has chosen dishes from all the countries that border the Mediterranean Sea—couscous from Morocco, Strawberries Romanoff from France, kabobs from Turkey, homos from the Middle East—all traditional Mediterranean dishes adapted to suit his taste. "This is my cuisine," Kassim asserts. "I cannot give you precise recipes for the dishes here because I cook on instinct, on feel, not by a cookbook."

Originally from Baghdad, Iraq, he immigrated to this country nine years ago at the age of twenty-three. Not lacking in confidence, he decided to go into the restaurant business after attending Donnelly College, confessing, "I knew I'd do well." He worked at several restaurants around town, including Plaza III, before opening the Olive Tree with a relative. When they went their separate ways, Kassim opened his restaurant this past spring.

Kassim's restaurant philosophy couldn't be simpler. "You have to serve good food," he propounds. "Service is important, and prices must be reasonable. But if the food isn't any good, what difference do the other two make? The food must be good."

8241 Wornall Road

HOMOS

1 (16-ounce) can garbanzo beans
3 tablespoons lemon juice
2 tablespoons tahini
2 cloves garlic, minced
Pinch of cumin
Salt
2 pieces pita (pocket bread), cut into rounds,
    squares or triangles and toasted
2 teaspoons olive oil
½ teaspoon paprika
1 tablespoon chopped parsley

1. In a blender, combine beans, lemon juice, tahini, garlic and cumin.
   Mix well. Add salt to taste.
2. Serve on toasted pita slices. Dribble with oil and sprinkle with
   paprika and parsley.

*This is a very common appetizer in the Middle East; it is eaten by kings
and peasants alike.*

AL-ROUBAIE SOUP

1 onion, chopped
3 cloves garlic, minced
1½ tablespoons butter
3 cups chicken broth
1 bay leaf
1 cup cream
¼ teaspoon white pepper
1 teaspoon horseradish
1 egg white
Dash of anise
4 teaspoons chopped olives

1. Sauté the onion and garlic in butter until the onion is transparent.
2. Add onions and garlic to the broth along with all of the remaining ingredients except the olives. Simmer 30 minutes. Remove the bay leaf and strain the broth.
3. Serve hot with a teaspoon of chopped olives on top of each serving.

This soup is my own creation. The horseradish and the anise give it an unusual, subtle flavor.

TURKISH LAMB KABOB

1 cup olive oil
½ cup lemon juice
1 onion, chopped
2 cloves garlic, chopped
1 bay leaf
1 teaspoon parsley
1 teaspoon oregano
1 teaspoon thyme
1 teaspoon rosemary
16 (1") cubes of lamb, cut from the leg
3 green peppers, cut into 1" squares
8 small boiling onions
8 mushrooms
1 zucchini, cut into 1" slices
8 cherry tomatoes

1. Mix together the olive oil, lemon juice, chopped onion, garlic and herbs. Marinate the lamb cubes for at least 6 hours.
2. On 12" skewers, alternate pieces of lamb with the vegetables. Broil the lamb skewers for 15 minutes, longer if you want your lamb well done. Serve immediately.

In the Muslim religion it is forbidden to drink liquor. In Iraq, you would drink buttermilk with the kabob, not wine.

POTATOES AL-ROUBAIE

2 large potatoes, cut into halves lengthwise
1 cup chicken broth
½ onion, chopped
½ green pepper, chopped
1 clove garlic, pressed
1 teaspoon turmeric
Salt to taste

Place all ingredients in a saucepan and bring to a boil. Cover, reduce heat and simmer for 30 minutes. Serve ½ potato per person. Spoon vegetables over.

This is a very simple recipe, but you will be surprised at how good the potatoes are. They go with practically everything.

STRAWBERRIES ROMANOFF

4 scoops vanilla ice cream
2 ounces brandy
2 ounces Grand Marnier
1 cup whipped cream, sweetened with
    confectioners' sugar to taste
12 fresh strawberries

Place 1 scoop of ice cream in each of 4 dessert glasses. Pour ½ ounce each of brandy and Grand Marnier over ice cream. Top with whipped cream and strawberries.

This dessert goes exceptionally well with highly seasoned food.

Dinner for Six

James Beard's Clam Soup That Cures

Peppered Duck with Figs in Red Port Sauce

Sugar Snap Peas

Boston Bibb Lettuce with Soy-Sesame Vinaigrette

Sugarbush Mountain Maple Mousse

Wines:

With Soup—Mirassou Chardonnay, 1978
With Duck—Beaulieu Vineyards Cabernet Sauvignon,
1976

Bradley Ogden, Chef
Byron Byron, Host

Most people, if they heard that a restaurant was serving American food, would without hesitation imagine the menu to consist of fried chicken, cheeseburgers, barbecued ribs, onion rings and apple pie. They would also be mistaken in the case of the American Restaurant.

The American Restaurant, perched on top of Hall's at Crown Center, has a better idea. It serves gourmet American cuisine, offering to the hungry nationalist dishes like Northwest Salmon Quenelles with Snails in Cream Sauce or Tartlet of Kentucky Ham and Brie. "We want to prepare American food with a European flair," asserts Brad Ogden, the chef at the American. "We are employing a lot of European-derived techniques, especially the use of fresh stocks and sauces, in combination with American recipes."

Moreover, most people, if they heard that an architect had designed an American restaurant, would surely imagine the interior to resemble a colonial dining room or a frontiersman's rugged cabin. In surprise, they would marvel at what New Haven architect Warren Platner has done for the American Restaurant. The American is spectacular. The ceiling in the main dining room, which is over three stories high, is covered with a fan-shaped network of wood and clear lights. The carpeting, the shutters on the ceiling-high windows, and the napery are shades of beige, all highlighted by scarlet banquettes.

Yet, as beautiful as the restaurant is, the emphasis falls on the food. Ogden, a graduate of the Culinary Institute of America, relates, "People dine out for the food first, the atmosphere and service second. Our food has to be good to attract customers."

200 East 25th Street

JAMES BEARD'S CLAM SOUP THAT CURES

24 fresh clams, well scrubbed
4½ cups half and half
Pinches of salt and cayenne pepper

1. Remove clams from their shells, being sure to reserve their liquid.
2. Heat the half and half with the salt and cayenne. Bring to a boil.
3. Immediately add the clams and their juice and bring the soup to
   boil again. Serve.

Note: We use cherrystone clams for this soup. We don't chop them
because the whole clam looks better than the chopped. Be careful not
to overcook the clams as they will get tough and stringy; as soon as
the soup boils, serve it.

PEPPERED DUCK WITH FIGS IN RED PORT SAUCE

3 Long Island ducks
5 tablespoons kosher salt
¼ cup cracked pepper
2 tablespoons rosemary
3 cloves fresh garlic
2 tablespoons paprika
Figs in Red Port Sauce

1. Thaw the ducks in the refrigerator where they will not bleed as much as they would at room temperature. When thawed, remove their wrappings. Dry them on wire racks in the refrigerator for 2 days. This drying insures a crisp skin.
2. After the ducks have dried well, season them with the salt, pepper, rosemary, garlic and paprika.
3. Roast the ducks for 1 hour at 350°.
4. Turn the oven down to 275° and continue cooking for 30 minutes. This slow cooking will render the excess fat.
5. Let the ducks cool. Bone them: first quarter the ducks, then remove all the bones except the drumsticks, which you need to retain the shape of the quarter.
6. Before serving, reheat the ducks in a 400° oven for 5 minutes. Crisp them for 10 seconds or so under the broiler. Serve with **Figs in Red Port Sauce.**

Figs in Red Port Sauce

4 dry figs
2 cups port
Duck bones from the 3 ducks
1 carrot, coarsely chopped
1 stalk celery, coarsely chopped
1 onion, coarsely chopped
2 cups beef broth
¼ cup sugar
Juice and julienned zests of 2 lemons
1 tablespoon cornstarch dissolved in 1 tablespoon port

1. Soak the figs in the port overnight. When ready to make the sauce, remove the figs and cut them into julienne strips. Reserve the port.
2. Simmer the duck bones and vegetables in beef broth for 2 to 3 hours. Strain stock and combine with port.

3. Reduce the port and duck broth by half. When reduced, add the sugar, the lemon juice and zests, the figs and the cornstarch mixture to thicken. Taste for seasoning.

Note: Although this dish requires a number of steps and is a fairly complicated recipe, it lends itself to ahead-of-time preparation. You can pre-roast the duck hours or even a day before the final 10-minute roasting and short broiling. The sweet sauce complements the duck well.

SUGAR SNAP PEAS

4 tablespoons unsalted butter
1½ pounds sugar snap peas, strings removed
Kosher salt
Freshly ground pepper

1. Heat the butter in a skillet or a wok. Add the peas and cook, stirring, until barely done.
2. Season to taste with salt and pepper.

We like to use kosher salt because it contains fewer chemicals and has a better flavor than iodized salt. We are trying to serve food as naturally as possible.

BOSTON BIBB LETTUCE WITH SOY-SESAME VINAIGRETTE

¼ cup olive oil
2½ tablespoons tarragon vinegar
2½ teaspoons Japanese soy sauce
Scant ⅛ teaspoon oriental sesame oil
⅛ teaspoon coarse kosher salt
Freshly ground black pepper
⅛ teaspoon dry mustard
¼ teaspoon fresh or dried tarragon leaves,
   chopped and tightly packed
2 to 3 heads Boston Bibb lettuce, cleaned,
   dried and torn in bite-size pieces

Combine all the ingredients for the dressing and mix well. Toss with the lettuce to coat each leaf just before serving.

It is better to tear than cut the lettuce. It bruises less and stays crisp.

SUGARBUSH MOUNTAIN MAPLE MOUSSE

1½ tablespoons Knox gelatin
½ cup warm water
1 cup maple syrup
2 teaspoons maple extract
4 eggs, separated
½ cup brown sugar
2 cups heavy cream
1½ teaspoons vanilla
Vanilla Cream Rum Sauce

1. Soak gelatin in the water to dissolve it. Heat the solution over a double boiler so the gelatin dissolves thoroughly, then remove from the heat.
2. Add the maple syrup and extract to the gelatin mixture.
3. Add the egg yolks and heat in a saucepan, stirring constantly until mixture thickens slightly or coats the back of a spoon.
4. Remove from the heat and add the brown sugar. Let cool.
5. Beat egg whites until fluffy and forming soft peaks. Fold into the gelatin mixture.
6. Whip heavy cream with the vanilla to form soft peaks and fold into the gelatin mixture. Pour into a mold. Chill for 4 to 5 hours.
7. When ready to serve, unmold by dipping mold in hot water and then reversing it on a serving plate. Serve each portion with **Vanilla Cream Rum Sauce.**

Vanilla Cream Rum Sauce

1 cup heavy cream
1 cup milk
2 tablespoons dark rum
¼ cup plus 2 tablespoons sugar
2 egg yolks
1 teaspoon vanilla
2 teaspoons cornstarch
½ teaspoon salt

1. Heat cream, milk and rum in a double boiler until steaming.
2. Combine remaining ingredients and slowly add to the hot cream mixture. Let cook for 5 minutes or until thickened. Cool and serve with mousse.

Note: When you add the egg mixture to the cream, it is important to temper it first. To temper the eggs, heat them somewhat by spooning some of the cream mixture into them. This reduces the chances of scrambling the eggs when adding them to the hot cream mixture.

LA BONNE AUBERGE

Dinner for Six

Mousse de Saumon aux Ecrevisses

Sorbet au Champagne

Côtes de Veau aux Morilles

Tomate aux Concombres à la Crème

Timbale Elysée

Wines:

With Mousse—a Chablis
With Veal—a Médoc

Gus Riedi, Owner and Chef

"It has been a struggle," recounts an amused Gus Riedi, speaking of his fervent efforts to operate an outstanding French restaurant in Kansas City. The chef-owner of La Bonne Auberge, Gus, like a Swiss Horatio Alger, started at the bottom. When he arrived in Kansas City, a penniless foreigner, he spoke fluent French and German, but no English; and although he had apprenticed as a chef in Switzerland at sixteen, his first job in town at the Muehlbach Hotel required that he merely peel Dover Sole and cut onions throughout the day.

After the Muehlbach he worked in a number of restaurants, among them the Kansas City Club and Le Châteaubriand, before opening a coffee shop in North Kansas City. "That was all I could afford back then," remembers Gus, a highly skilled chef who can make pâte en croute in his sleep. "We had a steam table and made sandwiches. It was really something." In time he converted the coffee shop to a French restaurant. Since then he has been steadily improving the quality of his restaurant, and he now feels he will overcome his history of bad locations in his new 51st and Main quarters.

The new La Bonne Auberge serves many nouvelle cuisine dishes, which Gus characterizes as lighter, simpler fare than traditional French food. "Nouvelle cuisine has thinner sauces with little or no starch, unusual combinations of food, slightly underdone vegetables and carefully arranged oversize plates."

Yet, while his cooking may change, Gus has not. "I still want to have an excellent French restaurant, as good as any in Chicago or New York. We're about there."

51st and Main

MOUSSE DE SAUMON AUX ECREVISSES

6 large shrimp, shelled and cleaned (reserve shells)
¾ pound salmon
Salt and white pepper
2 egg whites
1½ cups cream
Shrimp Sauce

1. Preheat oven to 350°. Butter 6 individual soufflé ramekins. Cube the raw shrimp and salmon. Season both with salt and pepper.
2. Put the salmon in a food processor. As you process it, add the egg whites, then slowly add the cream. If necessary, add more seasoning to taste.
3. Fold the cubed shrimp into the salmon mixture. Spoon the mousse into the ramekins.
4. Place the ramekins in a pan of almost-boiling water. (The water should come halfway up the sides of the ramekins.) Cover loosely with foil and bake 12 to 15 minutes. Test for doneness by inserting a toothpick into the mousse. If it comes out clean, the mousse has cooked enough.
5. Unmold the mousse and serve with **Shrimp Sauce**.

The fresher the salmon, the greater its binding power and the more cream it will hold. The more cream it holds, the smoother the mousse. The cream should be very cold for this recipe so that the salmon can hold it more easily.

Shrimp Sauce

6 shrimp shells (from salmon mousse), or
   more if available
1½ tablespoons butter
1 teaspoon tomato paste
1 shallot, minced
¼ cup white wine
½ cup clam juice
1 cup cream
1 teaspoon lemon juice

1. Sauté the shells in butter until they are rose-colored. Add the tomato paste and shallot.
2. Add the wine and clam juice. Reduce by half. Strain the liquid into another saucepan.
3. Add cream to shrimp liquid and reduce the sauce to a syrup consistency.
4. Taste for seasoning. Add salt if necessary, but be careful with it because the clam juice is salty. Stir in the lemon juice.

SORBET AU CHAMPAGNE

2 cups water
1 cup sugar
Peel of ½ lemon
2 tablespoons lemon juice
1 bottle of champagne

1. Combine water, sugar, lemon peel and juice. Stir over low heat until sugar is dissolved. Bring to a boil and boil for 5 minutes. Cool for 2 hours. Strain out the peel.
2. Add half the champagne (keeping the other half well corked in the ice box or on ice) and freeze the mixture in an ice-cream freezer according to the manufacturer's instructions.
3. Place in a closed container and set in the freezer for about 2 hours.
4. Serve in cooled wine glasses. Pour the rest of the champagne over.

This amount of sorbet is too much for six people but in my opinion it would be very hard to freeze a smaller quantity. Sorbet served in this manner takes the place of what used to be called the "trou du milieu" or a refreshing respite between courses. It played a more important role when dinners consisted of ten to twelve courses.

COTES DE VEAU AUX MORILLES

3 ounces dried morilles (mushrooms)
6 veal chops, cut thick—at least ½", preferably ¾"
Flour seasoned with salt and pepper
4 tablespoons clarified butter
1 tablespoon finely minced shallots
¼ cup brandy
½ cup white wine
¾ cup cream

1. Soak the mushrooms in several changes of cold water, gently washing them after they have softened. (Grit usually clings to them.) Cut into bite-size pieces.
2. Dredge the veal chops in the flour. Shake off excess. Sauté in the butter about 3 minutes per side, making sure not to burn the butter. Remove the veal and keep warm.
3. Add the shallots to pan. As soon as they cease foaming, add the brandy. Reduce mixture by half.
4. Add the wine and again reduce by half. Strain out the shallots and veal settings. Add cream to the strained mixture. Reduce to a thick syrup. Add the mushrooms and bring to a boil. Taste for seasoning.
5. Return veal to the pan, adding any juices that the chops may have left. As soon as veal is hot, serve.

Note: The sauce should be brownish beige in color. The veal settings should provide the color. If they don't, add 1 tablespoon of a dark meat flavoring, like Kitchen Bouquet.

TOMATE AUX CONCOMBRES A LA CREME

3 large tomatoes, halved, or 6 small tomatoes
Salt and pepper to taste
2 medium cucumbers (burpless, if possible)
1 teaspoon minced shallots
¼ teaspoon minced garlic
Butter
½ cup heavy cream
White pepper
Juice of ½ lemon

1. Preheat oven to 350°.
2. Scoop out the centers of the tomato halves (or small tomatoes). Season shells with salt and pepper and turn upside down to drain.
3. Peel cucumbers, remove seeds and cut into cubes or shape them like garlic cloves. Blanch in boiling salted water and drain.
4. Sauté the shallots and garlic in butter. Add cucumbers to the skillet, then the cream. Cook until the cream has reduced to a syrupy consistency. Season with salt, white pepper and a little lemon juice.
5. Heat the tomatoes for 5 minutes in preheated oven, then fill with cucumbers and sauce. Serve hot.

Cucumbers are not usually served hot in this country but they garnish veal and chicken well.

TIMBALE ELYSEE

*Although this looks like a very complicated recipe, it really amounts to
a number of different preparations, which can be done at separate times.
For instance, you can make the génoise a day ahead or even a month
ahead and freeze it. The ice cream can also be made well ahead of final
preparation.*

¼ cup sugar
2 quarts water
Juice of 1 lemon
3 fresh peaches, skinned, halved and pitted
½ cup raspberries
6 tablespoons confectioners' sugar
6 **Génoise Circles**
2 tablespoons kirsch
6 **Almond Pastry Cups**
1 pint **Vanilla Ice Cream**
1 cup whipped cream made with 2 tablespoons
   powdered sugar
6 candied violets

1. Mix sugar, water and lemon juice and bring to a boil. Poach peach
   halves over low heat about 5 minutes or until tender.
2. Mash raspberries with confectioners' sugar. Strain.
3. Sprinkle the **Génoise Circles** with kirsch and place in the bottoms of
   the **Almond Pastry Cups**. Cover each with a scoop of **Vanilla Ice Cream**
   and a peach half.
4. Spoon 1 tablespoon raspberry sauce over peaches. Top each serving
   with whipped cream (using a pastry bag with fluted tip) and a
   candied violet.

(see next page)

Génoise Circles

4 eggs
½ cup sugar
½ teaspoon vanilla
1 cup sifted cake flour
4 tablespoons sweet butter, melted

1. Preheat oven to 325°.
2. Place the eggs, sugar and vanilla in the top part of a double boiler over hot but not boiling water. Beat with a wire whisk until the mixture is thick and forms a ribbon, 15 to 20 minutes.
3. Remove the egg mixture from heat and whip until cold. Fold in the flour and pour in the melted butter, mixing gently with a spatula.
4. Pour the mixture into a buttered and floured pan, about 10" square, and bake for 25 minutes in preheated oven. Turn out onto a wire rack and cool.
5. When cool, cut into ½" thick circles to fit bottoms of pastry cup.

Almond Pastry Cups

6 ounces almond paste
½ cup sugar
½ cup all-purpose flour
¼ cup milk
2 egg whites, lightly whipped

1. Preheat oven to 350°.
2. Mix almond paste, sugar, flour and milk. Fold in egg whites.
3. With the back of a spoon, spread 6 rounds of dough as thin as possible, 5" to 6" in diameter, on a buttered and floured baking sheet. Bake 7 to 10 minutes, or until golden brown, in preheated oven.
4. Immediately remove circles one at a time with a spatula, pressing each gently into the bottom of a dessert cup or compote glass. Work as quickly as possible because the pastry loses its flexibility in minutes. When cool, remove from glasses.

Vanilla Ice Cream

½ cup milk
1 cup heavy cream
1 vanilla bean
5 egg yolks
¼ cup sugar
Pinch of salt

1. Bring milk and cream to a boil. Cover and remove from heat.
2. Cut vanilla bean in half and scrape the insides well with a knife. Place scrapings and husks in boiled milk and cream. Let stand covered about 10 minutes.
3. Combine egg yolks, sugar and salt; whip until foamy. Bring cream mixture back to boil and strain into egg yolk mixture. Return to saucepan and heat slowly, stirring constantly. When mixture thickly coats a wooden spoon (180°), remove from heat.
4. Sieve into a bowl and chill thoroughly in refrigerator.
5. Freeze in ice cream freezer according to manufacturer's instructions.

Dinner for Four

Steamed Clams

Vine-Ripe Tomato Slices Vinaigrette

Broiled Halibut

Pecan Pie

Wine:
Pouilly Fumé, Le Fort
or
Robert Mondavi Chardonnay

Alan Lamoureux, Chef

Entering the Bristol Bar & Grill is like stepping into old-world elegance. Heavily leaded glass in the doors at the entrance, a green and white tiled floor in the foyer, dark mahogany paneling, lush palms and intricate tin ceilings conjure up images of gentlemen of yore meeting for conversation, oysters, port and a good cigar. Rich green tones prevail throughout. The waiters, busboys and managers wear dark green aprons or smocks to complete this old-world atmosphere. Interesting paintings softly lighted, art objects, silver and antique-styled furniture add to the Edwardian air. The magnificent stained-glass skylight in the rear dining room once graced an old English office building.

The music is jazz—traditional and contemporary. The lounge draws the young business crowd to meet friends in the bar after work. The dining rooms attract more mature customers who appreciate the good food and can afford the prices.

Bristol Bar & Grill specializes in fresh seafood, flown in daily from the Atlantic, Pacific and Gulf coasts. Seafood kabobs and fish filets are broiled over an open mesquite wood fire, in full view of dining guests. Chef Lamoureux says, "The mesquite imparts a subtle taste without masking the delicate seafood flavor." Kansas City steaks are prepared in the same manner. Fresh lobster, crab, shrimp and mussels are also featured items. A big attraction in the lounge is the seafood appetizer bar where customers stand while enjoying the food and live entertainment.

Alan Lamoureux, chef at Bristol Bar & Grill, is young but well seasoned. He started working in banquet halls when he was in high school, was graduated from the Culinary Institute of America, and has worked all over the country in Gilbert/Robinson restaurants. He had been their Executive Chef for two years when they asked if he would like to undertake being chef at their new venture, Bristol. He jumped at the chance: "It was my chance to get back into actual operations. Cooking is what I got into the business to do." Alan is out on the front line cooking every day. His eagerness is typical of everyone involved with this exciting, new Kansas City restaurant.

4740 Jefferson

over the country in Gilbert/Robinson restaurants. He had been their Executive Chef for two years when they asked if he would like to

STEAMED CLAMS

2 pounds fresh littleneck or steamer clams, well scrubbed
2 tablespoons fresh minced garlic
2 (8-ounce) bottles clam juice
½ cup dry white wine
¼ cup clarified butter
2 tablespoons finely minced fresh parsley
French bread

1. Place the clams in a large pot and add the garlic, clam juice and wine. Cover pot and place on the stove to bring to a boil.
2. When the liquid boils, gently stir clams and add the butter and parsley. Cover the pot again and continue to steam until all the clams have opened. (Discard any that remain closed.)
3. Ladle the clams into large soup bowls and divide remaining broth over the clams. Serve with crusty, warm French bread.

Note: My personal favorites for this recipe are littleneck clams. They are sweeter, have less grit in them and have more eye appeal.

VINE-RIPE TOMATO SLICES VINAIGRETTE

This is a simple salad, but it is delicious and at its best if you do use beefsteak tomatoes at room temperature.

4 fresh leaf lettuce leaves, washed
3 large, vine-ripened beefsteak tomatoes
1 red onion, sliced into thin rings
1 cup **Vinaigrette Dressing**

1. Line each salad plate with a lettuce leaf.
2. Core tomatoes and slice each into 4 thick slices. Place 3 slices on each lettuce leaf in a shingled manner.
3. Place several onion rings over the tomato slices and spoon the **Vinaigrette** over the salads.

Note: It is important to use vine-ripened tomatoes for this salad.

Vinaigrette Dressing

This dressing is also delicious on hearts of romaine salad.

2 teaspoons salt
1 teaspoon crushed black pepper
1 tablespoon sugar
¼ cup red wine vinegar
1 clove garlic, minced very fine
¾ cup salad oil or olive oil

In a small bowl, dissolve the seasonings in the vinegar and add the minced garlic. Whisk in the oil slowly and incorporate completely. Mix well before serving.

If you choose to use olive oil, be sure it is of top quality. For happiest results, the olive oil and tomato flavors should not conflict.

BROILED HALIBUT

That most time-honored of natural stoves, the backyard barbecue, is still one of the most popular. Cooking over hot coals enhances the flavor of all grilled foods and seafood is no exception. At the Bristol we use only charred mesquite wood which has a delicate aroma all its own. Mesquite is difficult to find but charcoal will work as a substitute. However do not use hickory or oak chips—they would overpower the delicate fish flavor.

2 to 2½ pounds halibut, cut into 8- to 10-ounce
    steaks approximately 1" thick
Salt and pepper to taste
Paprika to taste
Oil

1. Have coals hot but covered by a coating of white ash.
2. Rinse fish under cold water and pat dry.
3. Sprinkle each fish steak with seasoning and brush well with oil on all sides.
4. Oil the broiler grid well and place the fish steaks over the coals, keeping the grid 4" to 6" away from coals. Broil the fish approximately 5 minutes each side, turning only once. When turning the fish, oil the grid again to avoid sticking. Serve immediately.

Only fat fish should be used for broiling, such as halibut, salmon, swordfish, tuna, mackerel.

A good rule of thumb: To avoid overcooking any fish, using any method of preparation, cook the fish at 10 minutes per inch of thickness of the piece of fish at its thickest point.

PECAN PIE

Crust

5 tablespoons lard
5 tablespoons butter
¼ teaspoon salt
1 cup flour
¼ cup cold water

1. Combine lard and butter.
2. Mix salt into flour and rub the flour into the lard-butter mixture until it resembles coarse corn meal.
3. Add water and mix lightly until water is incorporated.
4. Place the dough in a bowl and chill 1 hour.
5. Roll the dough out on a lightly floured table to ⅛" thickness.
6. Carefully place the circle of dough into an 8" to 9" pie tin. Trim excess dough and crimp the top edge.

Filling

3 eggs
1 teaspoon vanilla extract
$\frac{1}{8}$ teaspoon salt
¾ cup granulated sugar
1½ cups dark Karo syrup
2 tablespoons melted butter
12 ounces pecan halves

1. Preheat oven to 325°.
2. Combine eggs, vanilla, salt, sugar, syrup and butter.
3. Place the pecan halves into the bottom of the pie crust and pour the filling over.
4. Bake the pie in preheated oven for approximately 50 to 60 minutes.
5. Cool at least 30 minutes on a cake rack before serving.

Note: Check the pie at 50 minutes to see that the custard is shimmery. If you overcook the pie, the syrup and sugar crystallize and darken. The pie would still taste good, but it gets granular and loses some of its eye appeal.

Costello's Greenhouse

Dinner for Four

Deep-Fried Artichoke Hearts

Wedding Soup

Tossed Salad with Bleu Cheese Dressing

Seafood-Stuffed Zucchini

Greenhouse Forty-Three

Wine:
Round Hill Vineyards Chablis

Vince Costello, Owner

For Vince Costello it was a sudden transition from twenty years in professional football as player and coach to restaurant owner, but it is one he has made with great success. When he left the Kansas City Chiefs, he knew he wanted to be his own boss. Back in Ohio when he played for the Cincinnati Bengals, he owned and operated a boys' summer camp for five years. That experience taught him about selling, people management and food service so Vince's plunge into the restaurant business was not totally foreign. Vince is on hand keeping an eye on quality control of everything from food preparation and cleanliness to having the napkins folded just right. "I keep a daily list of customer complaints and go over them every evening to follow up and correct the problem right then. Take care of the quality, and the dollars will take care of themselves."

The asymetrical design of Costello's suits the unusual exterior of alternating horizontal bands of rough cedar and narrow strips of copper. The interior features plants, trees, wood and glass. Different elevations with small groupings of tables surrounded by low plantings give privacy to each area yet do not block the view of the overhead plants. The high ceiling and extensive use of glass lends a bright, sunny atmosphere to the restaurant in the daytime and an airiness by night light.

A varied menu including excellent prime rib, steaks, veal and lamb is available daily. A wide selection of fish, with a fresh fish specialty every day, enlarges the selection at Costello's Greenhouse. An artistically arranged, eye-appealing salad bar is one of the true highlights of dining at Costello's.

Live entertainment in the lounge has attracted devoted fans of each night's featured music. Monday is Dixieland night, and Saturday afternoon is reserved for Old Kansas City-style jazz jam sessions.

Vince's outgoing personality, energy and good management have made Costello's Greenhouse a wonderful addition to Kansas City's eating establishments.

1414 West 85th Street

DEEP-FRIED ARTICHOKE HEARTS

Deep-fried artichokes are the special appetizer of the day about once a week at Costello's. They are the most popular appetizer served.

4 cups bread crumbs
½ cup grated Parmesan cheese
1 teaspoon salt
1 teaspoon pepper
20 artichoke hearts, canned or frozen
Lemon Butter

1. Heat deep-fat fryer to 350°.
2. Mix bread crumbs, Parmesan cheese, salt and pepper.
3. Cover artichokes with mixture and fry until golden in preheated deep-fat fryer.
4. Serve with **Lemon Butter.**

Note: It is very important to have the oil hot enough to quick fry the artichokes. Put just a few artichokes in at a time to keep the temperature of the oil from dropping.

Lemon Butter

½ pound butter, softened
3 tablespoons lemon juice
1 teaspoon fresh parsley

Combine ingredients and blend well.

WEDDING SOUP

This should be called "Italian Wedding Soup" because it is a traditional feature of the midday luncheon following an Italian wedding. In Italy, wild dandelions are gathered and used in the soup rather than endive as suggested here. If you are feeling adventurous, try dandelion greens sometime. They give a slightly sharper taste.

6 ounces cooked chicken meat, diced
6 cups homemade chicken stock
Salt and pepper
6 ounces **Miniature Meatballs**
½ bunch endive, chopped
1 egg
¼ cup grated Parmesan cheese

1. Place chicken meat and stock in a saucepan over medium heat. Season to taste with salt and pepper.
2. Add browned meatballs and chopped endive. Bring to a boil.
3. Beat egg and Parmesan cheese together in a bowl. Add a little of the broth to the egg-cheese mixture and mix together. Return the entire egg-cheese mixture to the broth and whisk until eggs have cooked.

Note: It is important to prepare your own chicken stock to give this soup the proper flavor.

Miniature Meatballs

½ pound ground beef
1 egg, beaten
1 tablespoon grated Parmesan cheese
1 clove garlic, minced
1 teaspoon salt
¼ teaspoon pepper
½ cup chopped fresh parsley
½ cup bread crumbs
2 tablespoons butter

1. Mix all ingredients above except butter.
2. Shape them into miniature meatballs (no larger than 1").
3. Melt butter in heavy skillet. Sauté meatballs until golden brown.

Note: This soup freezes well.

TOSSED SALAD WITH BLUE CHEESE DRESSING

1 head Boston lettuce or any type of the
   freshest lettuce available
6 ounces blue cheese
2 cups mayonnaise
½ teaspoon dry mustard
¼ teaspoon salt
¼ teaspoon white pepper
2 tablespoons cider vinegar
½ cup oil

1. Wash the lettuce and tear into pieces. Dry thoroughly.
2. Crumble blue cheese in a mixing bowl, but do not mash to a paste
   as this will make the dressing too smooth.
3. Blend in mayonnaise.
4. Dissolve dry ingredients in vinegar.
5. Add oil to mayonnaise, beating constantly.
6. Whip in vinegar and dissolved seasonings.
7. Toss together with lettuce and serve immediately.

A wooden spoon works well to blend blue cheese and mayonnaise.

SEAFOOD-STUFFED ZUCCHINI

One of Vince's fellow football coaches first gave him the idea for Seafood-Stuffed Zucchini. After many changes Vince arrived at this delicious and popular entrée.

4 zucchini, washed
4 teaspoons butter
¼ pound fresh mushrooms, washed and finely diced
2 tablespoons finely chopped shallots
2 teaspoons finely chopped onions
½ clove garlic
½ pound shrimp, crab or mixture
2 teaspoons flour
1½ cups hot milk
1 teaspoon heavy cream
2 tablespoons sherry
1 teaspoon lemon juice
2 tablespoons lobster base
1 teaspoon celery salt
1 teaspoon ginger
Dash of paprika
Dash of allspice
¼ cup fresh bread crumbs
Grated mozzarella cheese

1. Remove seeds of zucchini if desired. Cut in half lengthwise. Steam the halves until nearly tender. Scoop out pulp of zucchini, leaving some to form case for the stuffing. You should have ¾ cup diced zucchini.
2. Heat 2 teaspoons butter and add mushrooms, shallots, onions and garlic. Sauté until onions start to turn brown.
3. Add diced zucchini and seafood and mix well over heat. Remove from heat to warm area.
4. Melt remaining 2 teaspoons butter. Add flour to make a roux. Cook 5 to 6 minutes, stirring so as not to burn.
5. Add hot milk and heavy cream a little at a time, stirring constantly so as not to lump. (Use a wooden spoon, not a metal one.)
6. Add sherry and seasonings.
7. Preheat oven to 350°.
8. Mix sauce well with seafood-zucchini mixture, blending by folding.

9. Add fresh bread crumbs to make a workable stuffing. Blend by folding.
10. Fill zucchini halves with mixture.
11. Top with grated mozzarella cheese.
12. Bake in preheated oven long enough to melt the cheese and warm the zucchini. Serve with your own rice pilaf.

Note: Lobster base is available in specialty shops, but chicken bouillon cubes may be substituted.

GREENHOUSE FORTY-THREE

Several of Vince Costello's chefs had a hand in creating Greenhouse Forty-Three. This final version won everyone's vote. It may be served as a drink or dessert.

12 scoops vanilla ice cream
1 shot Cuarenta y Tres liqueur
1 shot Kahlua
1 shot Amaretto
Whipped cream
Maraschino cherries

Blend ice cream and liqueurs until smooth. Top with whipped cream and a maraschino cherry.

Serve this in a hurricane glass for dramatic effect.

The
DINNER HORN
Country Inn

Dinner for Six

Fresh Red Apple Relish

Cheese Bread Sticks

Spring Broccoli Soup

Stuffed Pork Chops with Apple Corn Bread Dressing

Ginger-Glazed Carrots

Green Corn Pudding

Golden Pumpkin Muffins

Dutch Strawberry Trifle

Wine:
Bolla Soave

Bonnie and Richard Kellenberg, Owners

The Dinner Horn Country Inn is Bonnie Kellenberg's dream come true. Cooking tasty food and sharing it with her friends has been a joy for Bonnie since her childhood on a farm in eastern Missouri. She majored in home economics at Iowa State University, taught in the Kansas City and Parkville school systems for fifteen years and catered for parties and weddings for ten years. Throughout these years, her heart's desire was to open "Bonnie's Tea Room."

The Dinner Horn could hardly be called a tea room with its expansive façade, three large dining rooms and the Country Tavern, but it does reflect the woman's touch typically associated with a tea room. There is a coziness and warmth about the rooms and style of service that make one feel like a guest in the Kellenbergs' home. The Kellenberg family does, in fact, live in spacious quarters on the second floor of the Dinner Horn.

The restaurant is a new building in the Pennsylvania Dutch architectural tradition situated on a fifteen-acre wooded hilltop in Platte County, fifteen minutes north of downtown Kansas City. It has a seating capacity of 240, including the banquet rooms downstairs. While the building is residential in character, it is constructed to commercial restaurant standards. The name "Dinner Horn" comes from an 1873 painting by Winslow Homer depicting the lady of the house standing on her porch blowing a trumpet-like horn calling her men in from the fields for lunch. A reproduction of the original painting was painted by Kansas City artist Jim Hamil and hangs in the entrance of the Inn.

Bonnie says, "Our menu is based on the Pennsylvania Dutch tradition of seven sours and seven sweets at each meal. It takes about five courses to accomplish this. We have one price for dinner because if people ordered à la carte they might not get the seven sours and seven sweets." The Dutch relish cupboard, where customers help themselves, provides at least four of those sour and sweet tastes. The salad, hot muffins and choice of eight or nine entrées, combined with dessert gives more than ample opportunity to complete the delicious task.

The Dinner Horn Inn is family oriented. It offers well-prepared, graciously served American specialties in generous portions. As Bonnie Kellenberg said, "No one comes to the Dinner Horn expecting to lose weight."

2820 N.W. Barry Road

FRESH RED APPLE RELISH

5 medium firm red apples
2 medium dill pickles
1 medium onion
½ cup sugar
¼ cup white vinegar

Wash and core apples. Place apples, pickles and onion through the medium blade of a food grinder. Stir in sugar and vinegar and mix well. Refrigerate.

Note: This keeps for almost 2 weeks so it is ready for that extra touch to enhance any meal.

Apples, pumpkin and corn are basic Pennsylvania Dutch ingredients. Kansas City is in an apple-growing region with orchards in Weston and Chillicothe and we almost always have some apple dish on the menu.

CHEESE BREAD STICKS

2 packages dry yeast
1½ cups warm water
2 tablespoons sugar
½ cup salad or olive oil
4 to 4½ cups flour
1 teaspoon salt
3 egg whites, slightly beaten
Coarse baker's salt
Grated Parmesan cheese

1. Add yeast to warm water and add sugar. Set aside until yeast mixture activates. Add oil. Slowly sift in flour and salt, mixing until you have a smooth dough.
2. Preheat oven to 375°.
3. Roll out pieces of dough the size of pencils and twist 2 together. Brush with egg whites and sprinkle with baker's salt and grated Parmesan cheese.
4. Bake on greased cookie sheet in preheated oven for 20 minutes.

The recipe calls for either salad oil or olive oil but olive oil naturally gives the bread sticks a distinctive Italian flavor. Choose whichever suits your palate.

SPRING BROCCOLI SOUP

1 medium head of broccoli
4 tablespoons butter
¾ cup chopped onion
2 tablespoons flour
2 cups chicken broth
1½ teaspoons Worcestershire sauce
1½ teaspooons Tabasco sauce
¾ teaspoon salt
2 cups milk
1 cup grated sharp Cheddar cheese
¼ cup chopped fresh parsley

1. Cut broccoli into tiny florets. Cook in salted water until tender. Drain.
2. Melt butter; add onions and sauté until tender.
3. Blend in flour and gradually add chicken broth, stirring all the while. Heat slowly until mixture boils. Add Worcestershire sauce, Tabasco sauce, salt, broccoli and milk. Sprinkle in grated cheese. Stir until melted.
4. Serve garnished with fresh parsley.

Fresh broccoli is absolutely essential for this recipe . . . frozen just does not have enough flavor.

STUFFED PORK CHOPS WITH APPLE CORN BREAD DRESSING

6 (10-ounce) center-cut pork chops, thick
    enough to cut a pocket in one side
Apple Corn Bread Dressing
Salt and freshly ground pepper
3 tablespoons butter

1. Preheat oven to 325°.
2. Stuff the pork chops with **Apple Corn Bread Dressing** and skewer the
   edge with toothpicks to keep closed. Season with salt and pepper.
3. Melt the butter in a heavy skillet and cook chops until golden brown
   on both sides. Turn gently. Cook about 12 minutes.
4. Place in a baking dish and bake uncovered in preheated oven for
   30 minutes.
5. Before serving, spoon on hot **Tangy Raisin Sauce**.

Note: You may have the butcher cut the pocket for you for best results.

Apple Corn Bread Dressing

½ cup dry bread crumbs
1 cup coarse corn bread crumbs
1¼ teaspoons salt
¼ teaspoon freshly ground pepper
3 eggs, beaten
¼ cup chopped walnuts
½ cup chopped apples

Toss bread crumbs and corn bread crumbs together. Add salt and
pepper, beaten eggs and walnuts. Dressing should be light and fluffy.
Add apples last.

*This is a basic farm recipe that I remember from my childhood. It is
Pennsylvania Dutch in origin.*

Tangy Raisin Sauce

¼ cup brown sugar
¾ teaspoon prepared mustard
1½ teaspoons flour
¼ cup raisins
¼ cup red wine
¾ cup water

Mix brown sugar, mustard and flour together in a saucepan. Add raisins, wine and water. Bring to a boil. Lower heat and simmer about 10 minutes, stirring constantly.

GINGER-GLAZED CARROTS

2 pounds whole small carrots, peeled
1¼ teaspoons salt
½ cup butter
2 cups sugar
⅛ teaspoon nutmeg
¼ teaspoon grated ginger

1. Preheat oven to 350°.
2. Cook carrots in enough water to cover, with 1 teaspoon salt, until tender, approximately 12 minutes. Drain and set aside.
3. Melt butter and slowly stir in sugar, remaining salt, nutmeg and ginger. Stir until sugar dissolves and turns golden.
4. Place cooked carrots in a buttered baking dish and cover with sugar mixture. Bake for 15 minutes in preheated oven.

Note: You can substitute whole canned or frozen baby carrots in this recipe.

GREEN CORN PUDDING

2½ cups fresh or frozen corn
1 tablespoon sugar
1 teaspoon salt
⅛ teaspoon freshly ground pepper
1½ tablespoons flour
2½ tablespoons melted butter
3 eggs, beaten
1 cup light cream
½ cup dry bread crumbs

1. Preheat oven to 350°.
2. If the corn is frozen, let it thaw. Combine corn with remaining ingredients except bread crumbs and pour into a greased 1½-quart baking dish.
3. Sprinkle with bread crumbs and dot with butter before baking. Bake in preheated oven for 35 minutes.

Note: Milk may be substituted for the light cream but the dish won't be as rich.

GOLDEN PUMPKIN MUFFINS

This recipe makes 12 to 15 muffins.

2 cups flour
1 cup sugar
1 tablespoon plus 1 teaspoon baking powder
½ teaspoon salt
¼ pound butter
1 cup canned pumpkin
1 cup evaporated milk
2 eggs, beaten
½ teaspoon cinnamon
$1/_8$ teaspoon cloves

1. Preheat oven to 375°.
2. Mix together the flour, sugar, baking powder and salt. Cut in butter until mixture has a crumbly texture.
3. In a separate bowl, combine pumpkin, milk, eggs and spices; mix well. Gradually add dry mixture, beating until smooth.
4. Fill greased muffin tins (or paper-lined tins) two-thirds full. Bake in preheated oven for 20 minutes.

A helpful hint for this or any muffin recipe is to use a small ice cream scoop to measure the batter when filling the muffin tins. It will give you consistent-sized muffins.

DUTCH STRAWBERRY TRIFLE

It is a Pennsylvania Dutch custom to put the dessert on the table at the beginning of the meal. We chose to include this recipe because it looks so pretty in a crystal bowl if it is to be placed on the table at the outset of the meal.

Mock sponge cake:

4 eggs
2 cups sugar
½ teaspoon salt
1 teaspoon vanilla flavoring
2 tablespoons butter
1 cup hot milk
2 cups sifted flour
2 teaspoons baking powder

Topping for trifle:

1 (3-ounce) package strawberry gelatin
1 cup boiling water
½ cup cold water
1 cup strawberries

Vanilla pudding:

3 tablespoons cornstarch
⅓ cup sugar
Dash of salt
½ cup cold milk
1½ cups hot scalded milk
1 teaspoon vanilla

Whipped cream or whipped topping
Whole strawberries

1. To make mock sponge cake: Beat eggs, sugar, salt and vanilla until very light. Melt butter in hot milk; cool. Combine with egg mixture. Sift together flour and baking powder and add gradually to liquid mixture. Pour into greased and floured 13" x 9" pan. Bake in 350° oven for 25 to 35 minutes until cake tests done. Cool.
2. To make topping: Dissolve gelatin in hot water. Add cold water and strawberries. Chill until partially set.
3. Cube mock sponge cake and place in a deep dish and add topping mixture. Chill until firm.
4. To make vanilla pudding: Mix cornstarch, sugar and salt together in the top of a double boiler. Combine with cold milk. Gradually add hot milk. Cook in double boiler, stirring until thick. Cover and cook 15 to 20 minutes. Add vanilla. Cool.
5. Pour the cooled pudding mixture on the set gelatin. Chill until firm.
6. When nearly ready to serve, swirl on whipped cream or whipped topping. Top with fresh whole strawberries.

Note: If you use frozen strawberries in their own syrup then do not add ½ cup water.

Dinner for Six

Bookbinder Soup

Oysters Rockefeller

Sautéed Breast of Chicken Kiev

Twice-Baked Potato

Medley of Garden Vegetables

Strawberries with Sour Cream and Brown Sugar

Wines:

With the Soup and Oysters—Hans Kornell Brut
Champagne
With Chicken—Rutherford Hill Chardonnay, 1978
With Strawberries—Schloss Vollrads 1976 Auslese

Cliff Bath, Owner
Joe Mercier, General Manager
Bill Kerwood, Chef

The entrance to Harry Starker's resembles a Roman baroque church grafted on a Mississippi plantation, an effect that derives from the spectacular stained-glass dome which lights up the restaurant's lobby as well as the impressively wide oval staircase. "Glass domes are the new rage in commercial aesthetics," remarked Cliff Bath, who owns and operates Harry Starker's.

However, practicality as much as aesthetics guided his recent remodeling. "Normally two-level restaurants are a no-no. People don't like to move up and down levels. The dome and the staircase draw people up. They are intrigued to see what's up there."

While the entrance hints of Rome and Mississippi, the rest of the restaurant, decorated with British artifacts, suggests a posh London tavern. In this spirit Bath named the restaurant after an old Englishman he happened on in a dictionary of biographical names. "I liked the ring to the name, Harry Starker," related Bath, slowly enunciating the syllables. "Plus, he was a jovial guy, known to consume large amounts of liquor and fine food. He rubbed shoulders with all sorts of people, rich and poor, and thus was a good model for my restaurant."

Bath learned his trade studying in the School of Hotel and Restaurant Administration at Oklahoma State and working nine years for Gilbert-Robinson. He opened Harry Starker's in 1972 and has gradually enlarged the menu from eleven to twenty-three items. The restaurant's original lunch and dinner service has expanded to include breakfast, a cocktail hour and nightly live entertainment.

Old Harry Starker would applaud Cliff Bath's style.

4708 Wyandotte

BOOKBINDER SOUP

Beurre Manié
2 tablespoons beef base
3 quarts water
1 carrot, diced
1 onion, diced
2 stalks celery, diced
1 tablespoon thyme
2 tablespoons marjoram
2 bay leaves
1½ teaspoons garlic powder
Juice of ½ lemon
Dash of Worcestershire sauce
1 cup tomato purée
1 pound red snapper, diced
3 hard-cooked eggs, chopped
½ cup half and half
1 cup plus 2 tablespoons sherry

1. Prepare **Beurre Manié** and place in refrigerator.
2. Add beef base to water in a large kettle and stir until dissolved. Bring to a boil. Add diced vegetables. Return to a boil, then reduce to a simmer.
3. Add seasonings, lemon juice, Worcestershire sauce and tomato purée. Simmer for 20 minutes.
4. Slowly add **Beurre Manié** to stock, whipping until smooth.
5. Add red snapper, hard-cooked eggs, half and half and ¾ cup sherry. Simmer for an additional 10 minutes.
6. Remove from heat and ladle into bowls. Lace each bowl with an additional tablespoon of sherry.

Note: You may substitute grouper for the snapper. It's cheaper, not quite the same quality, but of the same family.

This recipe is borrowed from a famous competitor.

Beurre Manié

¼ pound butter, softened
½ cup flour

Mix butter and flour together to form a dough. Form into small balls and refrigerate.

OYSTERS ROCKEFELLER

1 package frozen spinach, thawed and drained
½ cup chopped fresh parsley
1 bunch (approximately 8) scallions, chopped
2 stalks celery, chopped
2 shallots, minced
2 tablespoons anchovies
¼ pound butter
¼ cup Pernod
5 to 6 drops Tabasco sauce
Salt and pepper to taste
24 fresh oysters
Mornay Sauce

1. Sauté vegetables and anchovies in butter for 2 to 3 minutes or until vegetables are tender.
2. Add Pernod, Tabasco sauce and salt and pepper. Remove from heat.
3. Put into blender and purée.
4. Prepare oysters in half-shell fashion and place on baking sheet.
5. Top each oyster with spinach mixture and bake 5 minutes in 350° oven.
6. Remove from oven and immediately serve on napkin-lined plates.
7. Top each oyster with **Mornay Sauce** if desired.

It is important to serve hot oysters immediately after they come out of the oven. Because of their shells, they cool very quickly. The shells suck out the oysters' heat—that's why you often see them served on hot rock salt.

Mornay Sauce

4 tablespoons butter
¼ cup flour
3 cups milk, warmed
¼ cup white wine
2 tablespoons grated Swiss cheese
2 tablespoons grated Parmesan cheese
1 teaspoon salt
1 teaspoon white pepper

1. Melt butter in a pan until bubbly. Add flour and stir until smooth.
2. Add warmed milk slowly, stirring constantly to prevent lumping.

3. Add wine and continue to stir over medium heat.
4. In small amounts, add cheeses to mixture and whip until the mixture is again smooth.
5. Add seasonings and simmer for 3 to 5 minutes. If necessary, adjust consistency of the sauce with additional white wine.

SAUTEED BREAST OF CHICKEN KIEV

6 (7-ounce) boneless chicken breasts
6 tablespoons **Kiev Butter**
12 mushrooms, sliced
Flour, as needed
6 eggs, beaten
2 cups dry bread crumbs
2 cups salad oil
Kiev Sauce

1. Pound chicken breasts flat. Place 1 tablespoon of **Kiev Butter** on each chicken breast and approximately 2 sliced mushrooms per chicken breast.
2. Wrap chicken breasts around the butter and mushrooms with your hands, forming an oval shape.
3. Place chicken breasts on tray and refrigerate 20 to 30 minutes.
4. Cover each breast with flour, dip in eggs, then cover with bread crumbs. Refrigerate again 20 to 30 minutes.
5. Preheat oven to 375°.
6. Using a 10" skillet, add oil and heat pan. Test heat of pan by dropping a few bread crumbs into oil. Crumbs should foam. Sauté breasts to a golden brown, turning often to prevent them from burning. Appox 8 min.
7. Place breasts in preheated oven and cook for 12 to 14 minutes.
8. Pour **Kiev Sauce** over individual chicken breasts to serve.

Kiev Butter

¼ pound plus 4 tablespoons butter
1 tablespoon garlic powder
1 teaspoon black pepper
1 teaspoon flavor enhancer
1 tablespoon crushed tarragon leaves
2 tablespoons minced onion

1. Allow butter to soften in bowl. Add all ingredients, making sure
   they are mixed thoroughly into butter.
2. Chill until hard.

*Using "frozen" Kiev Butter enhances the flavor and moistness of this
recipe. As the chicken breast cooks, the butter only melts, it does not
disappear, and oozes at the touch of your knife and fork.*

Kiev Sauce

½ cup chopped onion
1½ cups sliced mushrooms
¼ pound butter
½ cup flour
3 cups milk, warmed
½ teaspoon chicken base
Pinch of salt
Pinch of white pepper

1. Sauté onions and mushrooms in butter until onions are transparent
   and mushrooms are tender.
2. Add flour to pan and hand whip mixture until smooth.
3. Stir in warmed milk slowly.
4. Add remaining ingredients, making sure the chicken base is fully
   dissolved. Allow sauce to simmer 3 to 5 minutes.

TWICE-BAKED POTATO

4 large potatoes (1 pound each)
½ cup diced onion
4 slices bacon, diced
⅓ cup instant potatoes
Dash of nutmeg
½ teaspoon salt
½ teaspoon white pepper
1½ cups sour cream
2 tablespoons chopped parsley
½ cup grated Parmesan cheese

1. Bake potatoes until done, about 1 hour.
2. Cut potatoes in half lengthwise. Scoop out potato halves into bowl, reserving 6 half-potato shells.
3. Cook onion with bacon until onions are transparent and bacon is crisp. Add instant potato to onion-bacon mixture. Combine with potato meat scooped from shells.
4. Add seasonings, sour cream, parsley and Parmesan cheese. Using hand mixer or potato masher, beat until smooth.
5. Generously fill and mold the 6 reserved potato shells with the above mixture. Sprinkle each with additional Parmesan cheese. Bake in 350° oven for 15 to 20 minutes or until golden brown.

Note: You might want to cook one additional potato in case one should break while baking.

I would not substitute for the bacon and onion, but you could add favorite things to the potatoes, varying the recipe. You need the fat from the bacon to keep the potatoes from getting too dry.

MEDLEY OF GARDEN VEGETABLES

1 pound carrots
2 heads cauliflower
2 bunches broccoli
Hollandaise Sauce

1. Slice the carrots. Cut the cauliflower and broccoli into florets. Blanch vegetables in boiling salted water for approximately 4 minutes. If vegetables are too crisp for your liking, additional cooking time is required.
2. Arrange vegetables on platter. Ladle **Hollandaise Sauce** over vegetables and serve immediately.

For your convenience, you can partially cook the vegetables ahead of serving, then shock them in cold water to stop their cooking and preserve their color. Before serving, you can drop them in boiling water to heat.

Hollandaise Sauce

6 egg yolks
½ teaspoon salt
⅛ teaspoon white pepper
1 tablespoon lemon juice
Dash of Tabasco sauce
¾ pound butter, melted

1. In blender, mix all ingredients except butter.
2. Slowly pour in butter while mixing on low speed, blending until thick and creamy, about 30 seconds.
3. Refrigerate if not using immediately. Otherwise, keep heated over warm, not hot, water until ready to serve.

STRAWBERRIES WITH SOUR CREAM AND BROWN SUGAR

3 cups strawberries
½ pint sour cream
3 ounces Grand Marnier
6 tablespoons brown sugar
6 sprigs fresh mint

1. Wash strawberries, remove stems and leave whole.
2. Coat strawberries in sour cream and divide evenly among 6 chilled wine glasses.
3. Float ½ ounce (1 tablespoon) Grand Marnier over strawberries. Sprinkle each with 1 tablespoon of brown sugar and garnish with fresh mint.

This is a delicious way to serve strawberries.

HOULIHAN'S®
old place

Dinner for Four

Mushrooms Escargot

Boston Lettuce Salad

Roasted Crisp Duck

Cauliflower

Bananas Foster Crêpes

Wine:
Robert Mondavi Chardonnay
Christian Brothers Zinfandel

Gilbert/Robinson, Inc., Owners
Warren Dobler, Chef

Tom Houlihan had a men's clothing store on the Country Club Plaza for many years. It was only natural when remodeling for the new restaurant at that location got underway that the delivery description for all the lumber, furniture, carpeting and equipment was "It goes to Houlihan's old place." Thus this restaurant with its novel menu and décor got its name. Houlihan's Old Place is the brainchild of Gilbert/Robinson, Inc. which is the outgrowth of a partnership of Kansas City restaurateurs Joe and Bill Gilbert and Paul Robinson. Nationally recognized, Paul Robinson is the recipient of numerous awards including the Ivy Award and several Outstanding Interiors awards from *Institutions*. "Houlihan's Old Place was an attempt to put together a coming new life style—a more informal style of living and eating. At a time (1972) when the industry trend was toward a limited menu, we went the opposite direction. We anticipated a market trend with our eclectic menu that appeals to appetites at 4 p.m., the dinner hour, or 10:30 p.m."

Houlihan's combines delightful and distinctive interiors with innovative, wide-ranging menus to provide a colorful and varied dining experience. Wood-inlaid walls and table tops, fabric ceilings and lush greenery create a natural, relaxed setting complemented by one-of-a-kind artifacts including Tiffany lamps, brass accents, stained glass, English pub mirrors and antique advertising art and posters.

Equally unusual is Houlihan's imaginative menu, offering everything from a light snack to full-course fare to Sunday brunch. The selection ranges from salads, sandwiches, burgers and steaks to escargots, roast duck and seafood. In keeping with the trend toward natural and nutritious foods, all items are prepared with the freshest ingredients available and light sauces, if any.

Chef Warren Dobler finds the Houlihan's menu a creative outlet for his culinary talents because of its wide variety. Dobler got his start working under a European-trained, German chef while Dobler was working his way through college in Bozeman, Montana. He later attended the Culinary Institute of America in New York. "We have an all-day menu that will satisfy anyone's tastes. With our variety and volume, it is a constant challenge to keep the quality up, but we have line checks throughout the day to be sure the best product goes to the customer."

Houlihan's bar and lounge areas are traditionally popular social spots. A loyal entourage is attracted by the bartenders' potent beverages as well as by an interesting assortment of specialty drinks such as the famous Houlihan's Cappuccino.

4743 Pennsylvania

MUSHROOMS ESCARGOT

16 large fresh mushroom caps (about the size of a silver dollar)
32 teaspoons soft **Escargot Butter**
16 extra-large whole escargots
½ cup bread crumbs
16 bacon squares, 1" pieces

1. Preheat oven to 450°.
2. Remove the stems from the caps of the mushrooms (reserve them for another use) and place the mushrooms cap side down in an oven-proof dish.
3. Spoon a teaspoon of **Escargot Butter** into each mushroom cap.
4. Place a whole escargot onto the butter pressing lightly into the cap.
5. Place an additional teaspoon of **Escargot Butter** onto the snail itself.
6. Coat the top of each mushroom with bread crumbs.
7. Place 1 bacon square on top of each mushroom and bake in preheated oven until the bacon is golden brown and slightly crisp.
8. Divide into serving dishes and pour the butter remaining in the baking dish over each portion.

Escargot Butter

½ pound butter, room temperature
3 tablespoons minced parsley
2 tablespoons finely minced onion
1 teaspoon black pepper
1½ tablespoons fresh minced garlic
1 tablespoon fresh lemon juice

Combine butter with parsley and onion. Add seasonings and blend until well incorporated.

BOSTON LETTUCE SALAD

2 small heads Boston lettuce, trimmed and
  washed in lightly salted water
1 tomato, cored
1 cup **French Dressing**

1. Divide lettuce leaves onto well-chilled salad plates in a neat,
   high-centered mound.
2. Make a small "x" on the bottom of the tomato with the tip of a
   sharp knife. Plunge the tomato into a pot of boiling water and
   blanch for 10 seconds (any longer will result in a stewed tomato).
   Remove the tomato from the boiling water and plunge it into ice
   water to cool. Remove the chilled tomato and peel the skin off.
   Quarter the tomato and place a wedge on each salad.
3. Before serving, spoon **French Dressing** on each salad.

*The tomatoes are peeled for the convenience of our customers'
digestions, but you may leave the skin on if the vitamins are
important to you.*

French Dressing

1 teaspoon salt
½ teaspoon white pepper
2 tablespoons sugar
2 tablespoons paprika
¼ cup red wine vinegar
1 cup salad oil

Dissolve seasonings in vinegar. Combine with oil and mix vigorously.
Chill. Mix well before serving.

*Olive oil may be used in place of salad oil, but will alter the taste . . .
suit your own preference.*

ROASTED CRISP DUCK

2 (4½-pound) ducklings
1 lemon, sliced
1 orange, sliced
2 cups celery tops and leaves
2 teaspoons freshly ground white pepper
1 tablespoon paprika
Sauce à l'Orange

1. Preheat oven to 350°.
2. Remove entrail package from duck cavity. Unwrap the entrails and place on the bottom of a roasting pan.
3. Cut off the duck wings at the second joint and place the wings in the roasting pan.
4. Arrange the lemon and orange slices and celery leaves and tops in a layer on top of the entrails and wings.
5. Add enough cold water to make 1" of liquid in the bottom of the pan.
6. Combine pepper and paprika and rub evenly over ducks. Place the ducks breast side down in the pan.
7. Cover the pan with foil and bake in preheated oven for 2 hours. Remove the foil and allow the backs of the ducks to brown, approximately 20 minutes. Turn the ducks breast side up and brown for an additional 20 minutes. When nicely browned, remove ducks from oven to a warm serving tray.
8. Strain the pan drippings and remove all fat before using in the duck sauce.
9. Serve with **Sauce à l'Orange**.

Roasting the ducks upside down (with the breast side down) allows the juices to run into the breast and keeps the meat moist and tender. Try cooking your Thanksgiving turkey upside down.

Sauce à l'Orange

Zest from 2 oranges
1 cup dark brown sugar, packed
2½ cups plus 3 tablespoons cold water
¼ cup granulated sugar
2 (8-ounce) cans frozen orange juice concentrate
¾ teaspoon ground ginger
½ teaspoon ground cinnamon
½ cup defatted duck stock from roasting
3 tablespoons cornstarch

1. Place the orange zest, half of the brown sugar and ½ cup cold water in a saucepan and simmer until the zest is tender.
2. Add remaining brown sugar, granulated sugar, orange juice concentrate, 2 cups cold water and spices to the cooked rinds and bring to a full boil, stirring occasionally.
3. Add duck stock and simmer for 30 minutes.
4. Dissolve the starch in the remaining cold water. Quickly whip starch water into the simmering sauce and cook, stirring often, for 2 minutes.

Note: Cornstarch makes a beautiful, clear sauce, but you must watch the sauce closely after adding the cornstarch because it will foam up. It is important to stir the sauce constantly at this point.

Use a vegetable peeler to remove the skin of the orange if a zester is not available, but be sure not to get any of the white part—it is very bitter.

CAULIFLOWER

At Houlihan's there is a fresh vegetable of the day depending on the season and availability. We are interested in retaining the vitamins and nutrients in the vegetables because our customers are interested in their health.

1 (3-pound) head cauliflower
1 lemon, cut in half
1 quart boiling water
¼ cup all-purpose flour
¼ cup salt

1. Clean the cauliflower and prepare for cooking.
2. Squeeze the lemon juice into the boiling water, then plunk in the 2 halves of the lemon shell as well. Add flour and salt to the boiling lemon water and whisk in. Simmer for 3 minutes.
3. Place cauliflower in boiling liquid, return to boil and cook 5 to 7 minutes. (This depends on how you trim and cut the cauliflower head. If you choose to cook the cauliflower whole, allow 12 minutes.) After several minutes, begin checking the core ends of the florets for doneness. Pierce with a fork or squeeze gently with your fingertips. The core should be slightly firm or al dente (crisp to the bite).
4. Serve immediately with melted butter or your favorite cheese sauce.

To cook cauliflower (and all other members of the white root and stalk vegetables such as potatoes, endive, celeriac and salsify) we employ an acid-based liquid to retain the whiteness. The acidulant cooking liquid is called a blanc (a French culinary term meaning white).

BANANAS FOSTER CREPES

1 pint vanilla ice cream
16 **Crêpes**
1 cup **Foster Sauce**, room temperature
2 bananas, peeled and cut into ½" slices

1. Divide the ice cream among the **Crêpes** and roll each to resemble a cigar. Place on a serving dish.
2. Pour the **Foster Sauce** into a skillet and heat to a full boil.
3. After the sauce comes to a foamy boil, add the banana slices and boil until they are just coated and warm.
4. Spoon the banana slices and sauce over each **Crêpe**. Serve immediately.

A decorative touch is to slice the bananas on an angle.

Crêpes

This recipe makes at least 16 crêpes.

3 eggs
2 cups cold milk
½ teaspoon salt
1 cup all-purpose flour

1. Beat the eggs lightly, then add the milk and salt.
2. Sift the flour into the egg mixture and whip into a batter the consistency of cream.
3. Ladle enough batter into a very hot crêpe pan to swish and coat the pan bottom with a thin layer. Pour any excess out of the pan.
4. Brown the crêpe on the bottom side, then turn it over and heat to just firm the second side. Repeat the procedure until no batter remains. Cool the crêpes before using.

Note: Chef Dobler strains the batter twice to avoid any chance of lumps. The crêpes can be prepared well in advance.

Foster Sauce

4 tablespoons butter
½ cup plus 1 tablespoon dark brown sugar, packed
¼ teaspoon ground cinnamon
⅓ cup honey
1½ teaspoons cornstarch
¼ cup banana liqueur
2 tablespoons dark rum

1. Melt butter in a saucepan. Do not brown.
2. Add the brown sugar and cinnamon and stir to incorporate. Cook the butter-sugar mixture at a boil for exactly 1 minute, stirring often to prevent sticking. (Watch the timing so that the mixture remains smooth.)
3. Add the honey, stir to incorporate and allow to come back to a boil.
4. Dissolve the cornstarch in half the liqueur and stir this into the boiling mixture. Whip in to bind. Cook 1 minute, then remove from heat.
5. Add the remaining liqueur and rum to the sauce, stirring constantly until all is blended.

Italian Gardens

Dinner for Four

Scaccia

Chicken Soup with Tortellini

Veal Potenza

Italian Spinach

Sammy Ciao

Wines:

With Soup—Pasqua Soave
With Veal—Pasqua Valpolicella

The founders of the Gardens—the Bondons and the Liparis—came to Kansas City from Italy in the 1800s and brought with them their superb original family recipes. They started the Italian Gardens in 1925 and moved to their present location in 1933. Its popularity was immediate and the word spread quickly that here was a restaurant which served authentic Italian specialty dishes. One of the secrets of their success was utilizing Italian women cooks, a tradition they still follow today.

The menu selection is so vast, it is said that you could dine at Italian Gardens every day for a month and never eat the same thing twice . . . actually more a modest statement than an exaggeration.

Since the late 1920s, Italian Gardens has hosted local and national celebrities: singers, dancers, pianists, comics and sports figures. It has been "the" place to dine and performers continue to gather there.

But for the most part, Italian Gardens is a family restaurant catering to hundreds of downtown office workers at lunch and the family "on the town" for dinner. The food is outstanding and the prices are extremely affordable—a combination that is rare. The management is hospitable, ready to greet you with a smile and a handshake. The owners are devoted to making certain that every visit to the Gardens is a memorable one. As you leave, a glance backwards would reveal one of the owners waving a hand and saying a traditional *ciao* salutation . . . till we see you again.

1110 Baltimore Avenue

SCACCIA

The founders of the restaurant came from the province of Calabria in Italy. They brought with them this recipe. Scaccia is only made in Calabria; it is a provincial specialty. It is served as an appetizer here, a main course there.

Pizza Dough
Meat Sauce
½ onion, minced
2 tablespoons olive oil
½ clove garlic, minced
1 (16-ounce) can tomatoes
1 tablespoon basil
1 teaspoon oregano
Salt and pepper to taste
1 eggplant cut into ⅛" slices
6 tablespoons olive oil (approximately)
½ pound mozzarella, thinly sliced
½ pound Parmesan or Romano, grated
½ teaspoon crushed red peppers
1 egg yolk mixed with 1 teaspoon water

1. Prepare the **Pizza Dough** and the **Meat Sauce**.
2. Slowly sauté the onion in the olive oil until translucent. Add the garlic, then the tomatoes and seasonings. Cook slowly for 30 minutes.
3. Sauté the eggplant slices for a couple of minutes on each side in 2 tablespoons olive oil. As the oil is absorbed, add more. Season the eggplant with salt and pepper. Set aside.
4. Preheat oven to 350°.
5. Roll the **Pizza Dough** out into an oval 12" to 14" long and 8" to 10" at its widest point. Cover two-thirds of the oval (lengthwise) with the tomato-onion mixture, then add in layers the **Meat Sauce**, the eggplant, the mozzarella slices and finally the grated Parmesan and red peppers.
6. Fold the uncovered third of the dough over and then fold this doubled part over the remaining section (producing 2 layers of stuffing between 3 of dough). Seal seams by pinching the dough together.
7. Poke holes in the top of the loaf with a fork. Brush with the egg yolk wash for a good brown color. Bake in preheated oven for 1 hour.

(see next page)

Pizza Dough

½ package fresh or active dry yeast completely
   dissolved in 3 tablespoons tepid water (100°)
1½ cups all-purpose flour (preferably unbleached)
½ cup plain bleached cake flour
1 teaspoon salt
½ to ⅔ cup tepid water
1½ tablespoons olive oil

1. Add dissolved yeast to the flour, salt and water in a bowl. Mix and knead for a couple of minutes.
2. Knead in the oil. Continue kneading until dough is smooth and elastic. Let it rise to triple its original volume at a temperature of 75°—3 hours or more. Deflate, fold in thirds, replace in bowl and let rise again to almost triple—about 1½ hours. (This second rise may be completed overnight in the refrigerator.)
3. When completed, deflate the dough and cover with a plate and a 5-pound weight to prevent it from rising until you are ready to make the Scaccia.

Meat Sauce

½ onion, minced
2 tablespoons olive oil
1 clove garlic, minced
¾ pound ground beef
2½ to 3 cups chopped tomatoes
2 tablespoons basil
2 teaspoons oregano
1½ teaspoons salt
1½ teaspoons pepper

1. Sauté the onion in the 2 tablespoons olive oil until translucent.
2. Add the garlic and ground beef. When the meat has colored, add the tomatoes, basil, oregano, salt and pepper. Cook slowly for 2 hours, adding water if sauce gets too thick.

CHICKEN SOUP WITH TORTELLINI

½ chicken with giblets, back, neck and wing tips
2 tomatoes, sliced
2 stalks celery, leaves included, cut into bite-size
    pieces
2 carrots, cut into bite-size pieces
1 onion, chopped
1 sprig parsley
1 bay leaf
Salt and pepper to taste
20 **Tortellini**
2 quarts boiling salted water

1. Place chicken, vegetables and bay leaf in a 3-quart kettle. Cover with water and bring to a boil. Lower heat and simmer the soup, uncovered, about 2 hours. Allow to cool and skim off the fat.
2. Remove the chicken and giblets and pick the meat from the bones. Return the meat to the soup. Reduce the soup to about 6 cups.
3. Taste for seasoning and add salt and pepper as needed.
4. Cook **Tortellini** in boiling salted water for 5 minutes. Drain and add to the soup.
5. Simmer the **Tortellini** in the soup for 10 minutes or until tender. Serve the soup steaming hot.

(see next page)

Tortellini

2 cups all-purpose flour
1 teaspoon salt
2 eggs
2 to 4 tablespoons olive oil

Filling:

¼ cup minced onion
4 tablespoons butter
1 cup cooked chicken meat
⅓ cup grated Romano cheese
2 eggs
⅛ teaspoon nutmeg
Salt to taste

1. Sift the flour with the salt. Make a well in the flour. Add the eggs, 1 at a time, to the well, mixing with the flour and then remaking the well for the next egg. After the eggs have been mixed in, add the olive oil, as much as is needed to moisten the dough. Knead the dough until smooth. Let the dough rest for at least 1 hour.
2. To make the filling: Slowly sauté the onion in the butter until it is translucent. Grind the onion with the chicken in a food processor.
3. Mix the ground chicken with the cheese, eggs, nutmeg and salt and set aside.
4. Roll the dough out to a thickness of ⅛". Cut circles in the dough, about 2" in diameter. Place about 1 teaspoon of the meat stuffing in the center of each circle. Fold 1 edge onto the other, making in effect a half moon. Seal the edges with a fork. Twist the 2 ends of the half circles toward each other. (The tortellini may be frozen at this point.)

Note: To cut down on the preparations before serving this dish, you can make the tortellini ahead of time and freeze them, or make the dough ahead and freeze it, or make the soup ahead.

VEAL POTENZA

1¼ pounds veal cutlets, cut into 2" squares,
   ⅛" to ¼" thick
1 cup all-purpose flour
½ cup olive oil
1 clove garlic, chopped
3 medium green peppers, cut into julienne strips
1½ cups sliced mushrooms
Salt and pepper to taste

1. Dredge veal in flour.
2. Heat oil and add garlic, veal and peppers. Fry about 10 minutes.
3. Add mushrooms and heat until mushrooms are hot.
4. Season with salt and pepper to taste.
5. Remove meat and vegetables with a slotted spoon and serve.

Note: If you want veal to brown, sprinkle on a little water while frying in hot oil.

ITALIAN SPINACH

2 pounds fresh spinach, cleaned and stems removed
2 cups salted water
2 tablespoons olive oil
1 clove garlic, minced
Salt to taste
¼ teaspoon crushed red peppers

1. Boil spinach in salted water for about 5 minutes or until leaves are limp. Drain. Rinse in cold water to stop the cooking and retain the bright green color. Squeeze out excess water.
2. In a large skillet, heat the olive oil. Add the garlic, then the spinach, then the seasonings. Sauté until hot. Serve immediately.

Because spinach takes up so much volume, you'll need at least a one-gallon kettle. Because it shrinks so much in cooking, you don't need much water.

SAMMY CIAO

Per serving:

1 cup shaved ice
1 teaspoon finely ground Italian coffee
2 scoops coffee or vanilla ice cream
1½ tablespoons Sambuca
Nutmeg

Put ice in bottom of blender, sprinkle two-thirds of the coffee over the ice. Put the ice cream on top, then the remaining coffee and the Sambuca. Blend until thick. Serve in a fancy glass and sprinkle with nutmeg.

Note: Make each serving individually.

Dinner for Four

Fettuccine all'Alfredo

Tomato, Onion and Anchovy Salad

Lemon Veal with Eggplant

Brandy Alexander Mousse

Café Calypso

Wines:

With Fettuccine—DeSimone Castel Vetrano Bianco
With Veal—Fontana Candida Frascati

Jasper Mirabile, Owner

Almost thirty years ago Jasper's was a tiny mom-and-pop operation. In 1953 Jasper Mirabile and his father bought Rose's Tavern, a small, dingy neighborhood watering hole. They continued to serve drinks, but in addition Jasper's mother—long before the health laws prohibited it—would cook at home Southern Italian dishes redolent with garlicky tomato sauces and then bring them steaming to the bar. There, customers would eat with relish Mama Mirabile's home-cooked fare.

The restaurant is still a family operation. But now Jasper's has a new bar and three lavishly baroque dining rooms, distinguished by tables covered with pink tablecloths and plush scarlet chairs and banquettes. Jasper's mother had attracted such a following that soon the Mirabiles built a kitchen on the spot for her and subsequently hired a full-time chef. Business has not waned for twenty-seven years, and the Mirabiles attribute their success to family ownership and a meticulous concern for details.

In Roman splendor, the restaurant now serves Northern Italian food, which employs ample quantities of heavy cream, cheese and butter. "Bere, Mangiare Bene—Eat and Drink Well," the restaurant's motto urges, and at Jasper's you'll do both.

405 West 75th Street

FETTUCCINE ALL'ALFREDO

Fifteen years ago we had to give Fettuccine all'Alfredo away. No one knew what it was. Now everyone orders it—it's one of the most popular dishes on our menu.

½ pound fettuccine noodles
4 tablespoons butter
2 cups heavy cream
1 cup grated Parmesan cheese
Salt and pepper

1. Cook fettuccine in 2½ to 3 quarts of boiling water al dente (when the pasta is done but has a bit of firmness to it). Drain.
2. Heat the butter and cream in a pan large enough to hold the pasta. Add the pasta to the pan and heat thoroughly.
3. Add the cheese and toss gently, being careful not to break the pasta.
4. Add salt and pepper to taste.

Note: This dish is good with a lot of pepper. If you have used salted butter, be careful with the salt in the last step.

TOMATO, ONION AND ANCHOVY SALAD

3 large home-grown tomatoes
2 large red onions
16 anchovy strips
Italian Salad Dressing

1. Slice tops and bottoms off tomatoes and cut center portions into
   4 slices, approximately ½" thick.
2. Slice tops and bottoms off onions and cut centers into ¼" slices.
3. Lay 3 tomato slices on each salad plate. Place onion slices over,
   then top with anchovy strips.
4. Spoon dressing over and refrigerate at least 1 hour before serving.

*With tomatoes and onions, the center slices look much better on the
plate.*

Italian Salad Dressing

1 cup olive oil
5 tablespoons red wine vinegar
1 teaspoon oregano
1 teaspoon minced garlic
Salt and pepper

Mix all the ingredients together well. Let the dressing sit in the
refrigerator for a day.

*The key to this salad is twofold: good ingredients—especially good and
ripe tomatoes—and allowing the salad to marinate in the dressing for a
few hours so that all the flavors mingle.*

LEMON VEAL WITH EGGPLANT

8 slices veal scaloppine (about 1½ pounds)
Salt and freshly ground pepper
½ pound eggplant, peeled and cut into 8 (¼" thick) rounds
Flour for dredging
2 eggs, lightly beaten
1 cup fine fresh bread crumbs
½ cup plus 3 tablespoons peanut, vegetable or corn oil
1 tablespoon butter
8 thin, seeded lemon slices
1 teaspoon oregano
1 tablespoon chopped parsley

1. Pound the meat lightly with a flat mallet and sprinkle with salt and pepper.
2. Sprinkle the eggplant rounds with salt and pepper. Dredge in flour and shake off the excess. Dip in egg, then in bread crumbs. Pat to help the crumbs adhere.
3. Heat the ½ cup of oil and cook the eggplant pieces on both sides until golden. Drain on paper towels.
4. Dip the pieces of veal in flour and shake off excess. Dip in egg to coat each piece well.
5. Heat the 3 tablespoons of oil and the butter in a skillet and cook the veal, 2 or 3 pieces at a time, until golden. Turn and cook on the other side. Continue until all the meat is cooked.
6. Arrange the veal on a platter, slices slightly overlapping. Top each slice with an eggplant round and lemon slice. Sprinkle with oregano and parsley and serve hot.

Part of the trick to this dish is being careful that the veal and eggplant don't get too brown. With the lemon, the eggplant and the veal are to give off a golden effect.

BRANDY ALEXANDER MOUSSE

6 ounces semi-sweet chocolate bits
1 tablespoon instant coffee
1½ tablespoons cold water
4 egg yolks
1½ tablespoons brandy
1½ tablespoons crème de cacao
4 egg whites
½ cup heavy cream, whipped
2 teaspoons sugar
2 teaspoons ground almonds
2 teaspoons Kahlua

1. In the top of a double boiler, melt the chocolate bits. Add the coffee mixed with the water, stirring until the mixture forms a smooth paste.
2. Beat the egg yolks until they are a pale lemon color. Add to the chocolate mixture and stir until well blended.
3. Add the brandy and crème de cacao and stir until the mixture begins to thicken. Pour into a bowl and let the mixture cool.
4. Beat the egg whites until stiff and fold carefully but completely into the cooled chocolate mixtur .
5. Put the mixture into a pastry bag fitted with a medium-sized fluted tip. Pipe the mixture into 4 stemmed dessert glasses or into pretty cocktail glasses. Chill thoroughly in the refrigerator for several hours.
6. For the topping, whip the cream until thick. Add the sugar, almonds and Kahlua. Continue whipping the cream until stiff enough to hold its shape. Spoon the cream over the mousse just before serving.

CAFE CALYPSO

1 ounce Korbel brandy
4 ounces Kahlua
2 cups hot coffee
4 tablespoons whipped cream

In each of 4 (6-ounce) heat-tempered goblets, put a splash of brandy, 1 ounce of Kahlua and ½ cup hot coffee. Top with a tablespoon of whipped cream.

JENNIE'S
ITALIAN RESTAURANT

Dinner for Six

Tomatoes Sicilian

Garlic Toast

Linguine with White Clam Sauce

Chicken Breast Piquanti

Lemon Ice

Wines:

With Linguine— Fontana Candida Frascati
With Chicken—Antoniolo Gattinara

Thomas Barelli, Owner

Before the turn of the century, the commercial and political hub of Kansas City was at Fifth and Cherry. From Delaware to Columbus Park to the riverfront, the city bustled about its business. City Hall, the City Market and the courthouse were originally in this area. In the early 1900s an Italian community began to congregate here; immigrants settled in this area and established family businesses—many of which are still there today. City Hall and the courthouse were moved and the neighborhood has gone through many phases since those days.

In spite of these ups and downs, Jennie's has maintained a loyal following. Third- and fourth-generation customers still go to Jennie's for family dinners. In fact, serving families makes up about eighty percent of the business today. For this reason Jennie's grandson, Tom Barelli, rebuilt the restaurant in 1976 on the site that was originally Jennie's home as well as restaurant and modeled it after an Italian trattoria.

Jennie's also does a large businessmen's lunch serving upwards of 300 daily. There are three daily specials—a hot plate, a cold plate (fruit salad in the summer) and a pasta of the day in addition to their regular menu items. "Nothing pretentious, just friendly service and good food at reasonable prices," says Tom Barelli.

511 Cherry Street

TOMATOES SICILIAN

5 medium or 4 large ripe garden fresh tomatoes
½ teaspoon salt
¼ teaspoon sugar (optional)
1 clove garlic
4 to 6 fresh mint leaves
4 to 6 fresh basil leaves
Juice of 1 fresh lemon
¾ tablespoon high quality olive oil
1 teaspoon freshly ground black pepper
6 ounces Provolone cheese, sliced
¼ pound ripe green olives
Lettuce (optional)

1. Have tomatoes at room temperature. Slice in thick slices and place flat in a Pyrex dish.
2. Put salt and optional sugar in mortar. Add clove of garlic and crush with pestle. Add 2 mint leaves and 2 basil leaves and crush again. Work to a light, chunky consistency. Add the lemon juice and mix well.
3. Pour olive oil evenly over tomatoes.
4. Pour ingredients from mortar evenly over tomatoes.
5. Using a pepper mill, grind pepper generously on top of tomatoes.
6. Slice remaining mint and basil leaves in ¼" x 1" strips and mix together. Spread evenly over tomatoes. Cover with plastic wrap and refrigerate for 30 minutes.
7. Serve on a platter with strips of cheese and olives. (As an extra garnish, tomatoes may be placed on a bed of lettuce.)

The true Italian will dip his bread in the juice of this dish.

GARLIC TOAST

1 loaf Italian bread
3 cloves garlic, crushed
¼ pound plus 2⅔ tablespoons butter
¼ teaspoon dried dill, or more to taste
½ cup grated Romano cheese

1. Preheat oven to 325°.
2. Slice bread into thick slices, leaving them in loaf. Wrap loaf in foil leaving the top half uncovered.
3. Lightly brown garlic in butter. Generously spread garlic butter between each slice, saving a little to glaze after heating. Cover entire loaf with foil and place in preheated oven for 10 minutes.
4. Remove loaf from oven and unwrap top layer of foil. Generously spread remainder of garlic butter over top of loaf and sprinkle with dill and grated cheese. Brown in the oven for 3 additional minutes. Serve hot.

LINGUINE WITH WHITE CLAM SAUCE

1 teaspoon olive oil
¼ cup minced onion or 1 shallot, thinly sliced
1 clove garlic, finely chopped
2 to 3 cups chopped clams in juice
1½ teaspoons chopped fresh parsley
1 tablespoon salt
1 pound linguine pasta
Fresh cracked pepper

1. Add olive oil to skillet over medium heat.
2. Add minced onion or shallot to skillet and simmer.
3. Add chopped garlic to skillet. Do not let onions or garlic brown.
4. Drain clams, saving juice. Add clam juice to skillet. Add parsley and simmer gently for 10 minutes.
5. Add clams and simmer for 5 more minutes. Do not boil or clams will become tough.
6. Meanwhile, bring 3 to 4 quarts of water to brisk boil. Add salt and pasta. Cook 8 to 13 minutes, being sure not to overcook.
7. Remove pot from stove. Drain water. Do not rinse pasta.
8. Place pasta on platter and add clam sauce. Mix well. Sprinkle pepper over platter using a pepper mill.

There is no cream or milk in this sauce. In Old World Italian cooking one never mixes fish with milk products; therefore, only the clam juice is used to make the sauce.

CHICKEN BREAST PIQUANTI

6 (6-ounce) boned chicken breasts
¼ teaspoon salt
½ teaspoon pepper
1 cup flour
2 tablespoons butter
1 tablespoon shelled piñon nuts (pignolia or pine nuts)
1½ cups white wine
1 teaspoon chopped fresh parsley

1. Wash chicken breasts; remove skins and excess fat.
2. Add salt and pepper to flour and mix well. Dust each breast individually in flour.
3. Melt butter in skillet over medium heat. Add chicken and brown lightly on each side, about 4 to 6 minutes per side.
4. Add piñon nuts to skillet. Do not let piñons or chicken stick to skillet. Lower heat and add wine. Simmer lightly for 10 minutes. Add parsley. Remove from heat.
5. Place the chicken on a platter. Pour wine sauce and piñon nuts over the chicken.

LEMON ICE

1 egg white
2 quarts crushed ice
1 tablespoon salt
½ cup confectioners' sugar
1½ cups boiling water
Juice of 6 fresh lemons

1. Add sugar to 1½ cups of boiling water. Stir 4 to 5 minutes until you have a smooth syrup. Let syrup cool to room temperature in pan.
2. Add lemon juice (with pulp) to syrup.
3. In a 1-quart bowl, whisk egg white for 5 minutes. Add syrup mixture to egg white.
4. Fill a 2½- to 3-quart bowl one-third full with crushed ice. (For a quicker freeze, add salt to ice.) Place 1-quart bowl into larger bowl. Do not let ice overflow into 1-quart bowl. Push smaller bowl down into ice until well settled.
5. Beat mixture steadily for 15 minutes, allowing bowl to spin rapidly and syrup to spread around sides of bowl. Syrup mixture will slowly freeze to a fluffy light consistency.

Note: The ice will hold up to an hour in the freezer if covered tightly or wrapped.

La Méditérranée

Dinner for Four

Escargots Gourmands

Salade de Saison

Mignon de Veau Polignac

Crème de Celeri

Mousse au Chocolat Blanc

Wines:

With Escargot—White Quincy, 1976
With Veal—Château Cos d'Estournel Bourdeaux Rouge,
1972
With Mousse—Moët et Chandon Champagne
(half bottle)

Gilbert Jahier, Owner and Chef

For Gilbert Jahier, owner and chef of La Méditérranée, cooking runs in the family. His father is a chef in Orleans, France, where Gilbert grew up. His father feared that if Gilbert learned to cook at his knee the boy would be receiving special attention, so at age fifteen Gilbert was apprenticed to another restaurant. He worked there for three years.

Looking for better opportunities than those existing in France, Gilbert immigrated to this country at age twenty-three. He settled in Washington, D.C., and worked in such famous restaurants as Sans Souci and La Rive Gauche. Four years ago, in a move towards independence, he purchased a restaurant on Kansas City's Country Club Plaza. Here, in a fashion more typical of France than of the United States, he does the cooking while his gracious wife oversees the dining rooms.

The husband-wife combination complements the provincial flavor of the dining rooms. "We have tried to create a rustic-type restaurant here," says Gilbert, "—something like you'd see outside Paris. The paintings and the dominant use of the color red give the effect." It could easily be a restaurant in Orleans. Like father, like son.

4742 Pennsylvania

ESCARGOTS GOURMANDS

24 canned snails
2 to 3 tablespoons butter
Pinch of minced shallot
1 tablespoon Cognac
2 tablespoons finely chopped tomato
1½ cups heavy cream
Salt and pepper
Croutons

1. Sauté snails 4 to 5 minutes in butter and add a pinch of minced shallot.
2. Deglaze with Cognac and add tomato.
3. Add heavy cream and stir until well blended.
4. Season to taste and simmer for 5 to 7 minutes or until sauce has thickened enough to coat a spoon.
5. Serve with croutons.

Note: This is optional, but you can improve the flavor of the snails by simmering them for 10 minutes before the above preparation. Place the snails in a saucepan, cover them with wine and add ¼ teaspoon each of thyme and basil and ½ of a small bay leaf. Don't let them boil or they'll get tough.

SALADE DE SAISON

1 head of romaine, the outer leaves discarded, the
    remainder cleaned and torn into bite-size pieces
8 mushrooms, cleaned and thinly sliced
2 tomatoes, sliced
Vinaigrette
¼ cup chopped parsley (approximately)

1. Divide the lettuce among individual plates.
2. Place the mushrooms and tomatoes on top.
3. Before serving, pour on **Vinaigrette** and sprinkle parsley on top of
    each salad.

Vinaigrette

3 tablespoons Jerez vinegar
½ teaspoon Dijon mustard
1½ teaspoons chopped green pepper
1½ teaspoons chopped pimiento
1 teaspoon fresh tarragon, or ½ teaspoon dried
Pinch of minced garlic
Pinch of minced shallots
⅔ cup walnut oil
Salt and pepper to taste

1. Mix the vinegar with the mustard.
2. Add the green pepper, pimiento, tarragon, garlic and shallots and
    mix well.
3. Add the oil and season with salt and pepper to taste.

*Walnut oil is not commonly used for salad dressings here in the
United States, but it gives a distinctive and intriguing flavor.*

MIGNON DE VEAU POLIGNAC

Because the veal is mild flavored, it takes well to other flavors, like the Porto and raisins in this recipe. The other flavors actually help the veal.

4 (8-ounce) mignons of veal (a mignon is
    a 1" thick loin chop, boned)
Salt and pepper
3 tablespoons butter
1 tablespoon minced shallot
¼ cup Porto wine
1 cup **Demi-Glace de Viande**
2 ounces raisins

1. Season the meat with salt and pepper.
2. Brown each side quickly in 2 tablespoons butter. Reduce heat and sauté for 7 minutes on each side. Remove from pan and keep warm in a 200° oven.
3. Add minced shallot to the pan and deglaze with Porto wine. Simmer until reduced by half.
4. Add **Demi-Glace de Viande** and simmer 5 minutes.
5. Add raisins and remaining butter. Taste for seasoning and adjust if necessary.
6. To serve, pour the sauce over the veal.

Demi-Glace de Viande

This recipe makes 1 quart. You may freeze the remainder.

2 pounds veal bones
2 carrots, coarsely chopped
1 onion, coarsely chopped
2 stalks celery, coarsely chopped
2 tomatoes, coarsely chopped
½ cup white wine
1 tablespoon basil
2 teaspoons thyme
1 bay leaf
2 teaspoons salt
Pepper to taste

1. Brown bones with vegetables and seasonings in a 450° oven.
2. When browned, add to stock pot. Cover with water and add the wine and seasonings.
3. Simmer 5 to 6 hours. Strain. (You should have about 5 quarts.)
4. Reduce 5 quarts to 1 quart, skimming from time to time. Adjust seasoning.

CREME DE CELERI

The celery root, while common in France, is not too well known here. It has a spicy, peppery taste and goes especially well with game. You can obtain it here at some groceries.

1 celery root, peeled
2 potatoes, peeled
1 medium onion
Salt and pepper
1 teaspoon nutmeg
2 to 3½ cups milk

1. Preheat oven to 400°.
2. Quarter celery root, potatoes and onion. Arrange to fit tightly in a casserole.
3. Add salt, pepper and nutmeg and cover with milk.
4. Bring the milk to a full boil and immediately remove from heat.
5. Cover casserole and cook in preheated oven for 35 minutes.
6. Pass through a blender until smooth textured. Adjust the seasonings.

MOUSSE AU CHOCOLAT BLANC

Chocolate mousse made with black chocolate is everywhere. Mousse made with white chocolate is unusual. The taste is different, much lighter.

4 ounces white chocolate
1½ tablespoons water
2 egg yolks
½ cup sugar
1 pint heavy cream
Dash of Kirsch

1. Melt the chocolate with the water in a double boiler.
2. Combine egg yolks and sugar and slowly add chocolate mixture.
3. Beat the heavy cream until stiff and fold into the chocolate mixture.
4. Add a dash of Kirsch. Refrigerate before serving.

nabil's

Dinner for Four

Tabouleh

Cream of Avocado Soup

Romaine Salad with Mint Vinaigrette Dressing

Veal with Dijon

Chocolate Mousse

Wines:

With Tabouleh—Ouzo on the rocks
With Veal—Beaujolais-Villages, Louis Jadot

Nabil Saleh, Owner
David Scott, Chef

"It was a logical progression to European cooking," Nabil Saleh casually recounts of his opening Nabil's on the Country Club Plaza. The thirty-year-old restaurateur with a master's degree in Middle Eastern studies had previously worked on Wall Street. What could make more sense?

Actually, the pieces do fit together. Dissatisfied with New York, Nabil returned to Kansas City where he had lived since he was seven years old, his parents having immigrated there from Lebanon. Nabil had learned to cook in New York from a circle of culinary-minded friends. So in 1973, after his return from New York, Nabil opened Nabil's on Broadway, serving Middle Eastern food. "I did not have any confidence that it would go over," remembers Nabil. "I hoped a small foreign restaurant would get a portion of the non-steak-and-potatoes crowd."

The restaurant did go over and in 1975 Nabil opened another in Lawrence, Kansas. Not wanting to compete with his Broadway restaurant only a few blocks to the north, he decided to feature a European menu in this new restaurant. In the L-shaped dining room, decorated with plants and with rugs hanging on the walls, Nabil serves a wide assortment of Continental dishes, ranging from a fettuccine of the day to Trout Almondine.

While Middle Eastern cooking uses little meat and a lot of garlic and spices, European cooking is more subtle, using more wine and meat and milder seasonings. "The transition from one cuisine to another was easy," Nabil asserts offhandedly. Of course, it's only logical.

4735 Wyandotte

TABOULEH

½ cup cracked wheat
4 tomatoes
2 bunches parsley, finely chopped
4 scallions, finely chopped
¼ teaspoon dried mint
2 tablespoons olive oil
Juice of 1 lemon
Salt
4 lettuce leaves

1. Soak the wheat in water by placing wheat in a bowl and adding just enough water to cover. Let soak for 15 minutes. Drain.
2. Slice 2 of the tomatoes and set aside. Chop the remaining 2 tomatoes. Add to the wheat with the parsley, scallions, mint, olive oil and lemon juice. Season to taste.
3. Chill the mixture for 15 to 20 minutes and serve on lettuce leaves with sliced tomatoes as garnish.

Note: There are a number of different degrees of coarseness of cracked wheat. For Tabouleh the #2 cracked wheat is the best.

CREAM OF AVOCADO SOUP

This is an unusual soup which will intrigue your guests. Be sure your avocados are ripe—otherwise the flavor will not be strong enough.

2 large avocados, peeled and pitted
1 onion, coarsely chopped
5 to 8 stems parsley
1 small handful fresh, cleaned spinach
¼ green pepper
2 teaspoons salt
1 teaspoon white pepper
½ teaspoon Tabasco sauce
1 teaspoon Worcestershire sauce
1 tablespoon Le Goût chicken base
½ teaspoon Maggi liquid
½ cup cream
3 cups milk
⅓ cup sour cream
1 tablespoon lemon juice

1. Purée the first 5 ingredients in a blender or cuisinart. Mix in the remaining ingredients.
2. Chill approximately 3 hours.

ROMAINE SALAD WITH MINT VINAIGRETTE DRESSING

1 head romaine, trimmed, washed, dried and
   cut into bite-size pieces
2 medium tomatoes, sliced
1 large green pepper, sliced
4 scallions, chopped
Mint Vinaigrette Dressing

Gently mix the vegetables and chill. Add the dressing and serve on chilled plates.

Mint Vinaigrette Dressing

½ cup olive oil
Juice of 1 lemon
1 teaspoon dried mint
Salt

Mix all ingredients well. Let the dressing sit for a couple of hours before using.

VEAL WITH DIJON

1 pound veal scaloppine, pounded and floured
6 tablespoons butter
16 white mushrooms, sliced
1 cup sour cream
1½ tablespoons Dijon mustard

1. Sauté the veal in 4 tablespoons butter, about 2 minutes per side, not letting the veal brown. Remove the veal from the pan and keep warm.
2. In another skillet, gently sauté the mushrooms in 2 tablespoons butter.
3. Add the sour cream, mustard and mushrooms to the veal pan. Heat and mix well. Scrape up any sediment on the bottom of the skillet.
4. Return the veal to the skillet and reheat. Serve.

It is important not to brown the veal because the browning will dry out this delicate meat.

CHOCOLATE MOUSSE

This is a good dessert not only because people like chocolate but because it can be made a day ahead. The honey gives it a slightly different taste from the typical chocolate mousse.

5 ounces unsweetened chocolate
4 tablespoons butter
½ cup sugar
4 tablespoons honey
1 tablespoon instant coffee
¼ cup cream
2 egg yolks
2 tablespoons rum
2 cups whipping cream
4 egg whites

1. Place first 6 ingredients in a double boiler until chocolate is melted. Hold aside from the heat until the chocolate mixture is at room temperature.
2. Add yolks and rum to the chocolate mixture, mixing well.
3. Whip the cream; whip the egg whites until stiff. Gently fold whipped cream and egg whites into chocolate mixture. Pour into individual dessert glasses and chill 6 to 8 hours.

PLAZA III

Dinner for Four

Champignons Magiques

Steak Soup Plaza III

Broccoli in Hollandaise Sauce

Veal Sauté Smitaine

Strawberries in Plaza III Cream

Wines:

With Champignons—Pouilly-Fumé, Le Fort, 1978
With Veal—Robert Mondavi Chardonnay, 1978

Gilbert/Robinson, Owners
Phillip Hickey, Manager
Richard McPeake, Chef

The casually elegant, English atmosphere of Plaza III lends itself to relaxed dining. There are oriental rugs on parquet floors and hanging or potted plants all around. The restaurant is divided into separate rooms, each with a slightly varied atmosphere, but generally the restaurant is dark and quiet. In most of the rooms, large oil paintings hang on rosy brick walls. The table linens are pink and the flowers are in shades of burgundy, rose and pink giving the entire restaurant a rosy hue. Plaza III is sophisticated but not stuffy or formal. Manager Phillip Hickey says, "Plaza III is not a restaurant directed to a target market. It has a life history of its own."

Chef Richard McPeake graduated from the Culinary Institute of America in New York and was head chef in an upstate New York restaurant before coming to Plaza III. What he enjoys most of all is creating the special dinner of the week. He says, "I do a lot of research and get input from the other cooks, too. We love the opportunity to be creative."

The food at Plaza III is Continental but not complicated. The luncheon menu offers salads, hearty sandwiches, seafood crêpes, fresh vegetable omelets and specialty items. Dinner emphasizes a selection of Continental delicacies as well as roast duck, steaks and seafood. The wine list is extensive, and the service is attentive but not obtrusive.

Plaza III has won two Outstanding Interiors awards from *Institutions* and was voted one of the top restaurants in the country by *Sales and Marketing Management*.

Owner Joe Gilbert says, "There's nothing more pleasing than to see a customer who arrives hungry and grumpy go out with a happy expression. You've helped someone feel better. We're in the health and happiness business. If a place is not a success, you are not giving the customers what they want." Plaza III has obviously been giving the customers what they want because the restaurant has a large, loyal following.

4749 Pennsylvania

CHAMPIGNONS MAGIQUE

6 tablespoons butter
½ cup minced onion
½ cup minced celery
¾ teaspoon salt
¾ teaspoon pepper
¾ teaspoon thyme
¼ teaspoon dried rosemary leaves
¼ pound plus 12 (1") pieces Alaskan King
   crab meat
1 ounce dry white wine
2 cups dry bread crumbs
12 fresh, large 'silver-dollar-size' mushroom caps
Cheddar Cheese Sauce

1. Preheat oven to 350°.
2. Place the butter in a large skillet and allow to melt without browning. Add the vegetables and sauté until the onions are transparent.
3. When vegetables are tender, add the seasonings and ¼ pound crab meat. Allow to heat and add the wine and bread crumbs. Remove from heat and stir well. Allow to cool completely.
4. When the stuffing is cold, divide equally among the mushroom caps. Place the stuffed mushroom caps on a buttered baking sheet.
5. Place 1 piece of crab meat on top of the stuffing of each mushroom cap. Bake in preheated oven until hot and golden brown.
6. To serve, place 3 stuffed caps on each plate. Mask with **Cheddar Cheese Sauce**.

Cheddar Cheese Sauce

This is one of Plaza III's most popular appetizers.

1½ cups milk
¼ pound Cheddar cheese, cubed
¼ teaspoon paprika
¼ teaspoon dry mustard
½ teaspoon Worcestershire sauce
⅛ teaspoon salt
1½ tablespoons butter
3 tablespoons flour

1. Combine milk, cheese, paprika, mustard, Worcestershire and salt in top of double boiler.
2. Heat until cheese is melted and milk begins to form a skin.
3. Melt butter in a heavy saucepan. Blend in flour and cook 3 to 4 minutes over low heat, stirring constantly to prevent browning.
4. Add to hot milk-and-cheese mixture, whisking until smooth.

STEAK SOUP PLAZA III

This favorite has been on Plaza III's menu since its opening.

4 tablespoons butter
¼ cup flour
2 (10-ounce) cans beef consommé
¼ cup diced carrots
¼ cup diced onions
¼ cup diced celery
½ cup chopped canned tomatoes
¾ teaspoon Kitchen Bouquet
1 beef bouillon cube
¼ teaspoon ground black pepper
½ teaspoon flavor enhancer
5 ounces frozen mixed vegetables
½ pound ground beef steak, browned and drained

1. Place the butter in a soup pot and allow to melt without browning.
2. Add flour and stir to form a smooth paste. Cook the mixture (roux) over medium heat, without browning, for 3 minutes, stirring constantly.
3. Add the consommé to the roux and stir until smooth and lightly thickened. Bring to a full boil.
4. Add the fresh vegetables, tomatoes and seasonings and allow to regain a boil. Reduce the heat and simmer until the vegetables are just barely tender. (This should take about 20 to 30 minutes.)
5. Add the frozen vegetables and the browned ground steak. Simmer an additional 15 minutes.

Be sure to simmer long enough that the flavors become well blended.

BROCCOLI IN HOLLANDAISE SAUCE

1 to 1½ pounds broccoli
Hollandaise Sauce

1. Wash broccoli head well under running water as quickly as possible so excess water will not be absorbed. Trim leaves and cut into stalks. Using a potato peeler, peel stems.
2. Place broccoli in rapidly boiling salted water. When water resumes boiling, cook 5 to 7 minutes or al dente.
3. Serve with **Hollandaise Sauce.**

Hollandaise Sauce

½ cup egg yolks (6 or 7), at room temperature
¾ teaspoon salt
¼ teaspoon Tabasco sauce
¼ teaspoon ground white pepper
1 cup melted butter, at room temperature
Warm water
½ tablespoon fresh lemon juice (approximately)

1. In the container of your blender whip the egg yolks until very smooth, about 15 seconds. Add the salt, Tabasco sauce and pepper; whip another 15 seconds.
2. Turn the blender on medium speed and slowly add the melted butter a tablespoon at a time for the first half cup. As the butter is being added, notice the sauce beginning to thicken. Never allow the sauce to become thicker than cake batter or it will curdle (the yolks will discharge the butter they hold). If the sauce becomes thicker than cake batter, thin it down with a small amount of warm water, adding one tablespoon at a time.
3. Continue adding the remaining butter in a steady stream, constantly watching the thickness and thinning with additional water as needed.
4. When all of the butter has been added, add the lemon juice to taste and whirl again until evenly distributed.
5. Hold the **Hollandaise Sauce** at room temperature, covered, until you are ready to serve.

You may substitute concentrated lemon juice in this recipe, but use less of it because it is stronger than fresh lemon juice. The exact quantity depends on your personal taste.

VEAL SAUTE SMITAINE

The secret to this dish is to sauté the medallions lightly.

4 (6-ounce) medallions of veal
½ cup flour
½ teaspoon salt
½ teaspoon pepper
⅓ to ½ cup clarified butter
¼ cup scallions, thinly sliced
½ cup **Smitaine Sauce**
1 cup sour cream

1. Place the veal on a secure work surface and lightly pound each medallion with a meat mallet to flatten and tenderize uniformly.
2. Season the flour with salt and pepper and lightly dredge each piece of veal in the flour, shaking off any excess.
3. Heat the clarified butter in a sauté pan and allow to become very hot.
4. Sauté the veal in the hot clarified butter until golden brown on both sides, 5 to 7 minutes. Drain well and set aside, keeping the veal warm.
5. Drain off excess fat from the pan and reheat. When hot, place scallions in skillet and sauté 30 seconds.
6. Deglaze the pan by adding the **Smitaine Sauce** and stir in the sour cream. Bring the sauce to a boil, stirring to lift any drippings from the bottom of the pan.
7. Place veal on warm serving plates and spoon sauce over.

Smitaine Sauce

1½ tablespoons butter
3 tablespoons flour
5 ounces chicken consommé
Salt and pepper to taste
3 ounces heavy cream

1. Heat butter in saucepan. Stir in flour and cook roux slowly for 3 minutes over medium heat. (Do not let brown.)
2. Slowly whip in consommé. Stir until thickened and smooth and cook 5 minutes.
3. Add salt and pepper to taste, then the heavy cream. Bring to a boil and remove from heat.

STRAWBERRIES IN PLAZA III CREAM

3 cups whole fresh strawberries, hulled, washed and drained
1 cup **Plaza III Cream**, cold
4 whole strawberries, washed, stems on
4 fresh mint sprigs, washed

1. After preparing the hulled strawberries, divide equally into serving dishes. (Small wide-mouth wine glasses are preferred.)
2. Neatly spoon the cream over the mound of berries.
3. Garnish each glass by placing one whole berry (with stem on) and a mint sprig on top of the mound.

Plaza III Cream

½ cup heavy cream
1½ ounces marshmallow fluff
2½ teaspoons dark brown sugar, packed
⅛ teaspoon vanilla extract
½ ounce Grand Marnier

1. Place the heavy cream in a small chilled mixing bowl.
2. Add the marshmallow fluff, brown sugar and vanilla extract. Using a whisk, whip the mixture briskly until slightly thickened. (An electric mixer can be used.)
3. After the cream has begun to thicken, add the Grand Marnier and beat rapidly until the mixture thickens, but do not whip until stiff.

What makes this dessert so light and refreshing is that the cream is not stiff. The cream should be the consistency of honey.

PRINCESS GARDEN

Dinner for Four

Crab Rangoon

Seafood Hot and Sour Soup

Shrimp and Broccoli with Wine Sauce

Szechuan Spiced Shredded Beef

Toffee Pineapple

Beverage:
Tseng-Tao Beer or Chinese Tea

Chuen Look Chang, Owner and Chef

Princess Garden is a family affair. The Changs are everywhere. They greet you at the door. They seat you at your table. They pour your drinks. They stir-fry your food. They ring up your bill. They are the key to the restaurant's popularity. "The main reason for the success of our restaurant is that it is family owned and operated," confides Robert Chang, manager of the restaurant and oldest son of chef-owner Chuen Look Chang. "My mother and father, my brother, my three sisters, my two brothers-in-law—everyone works for the good of the restaurant."

The Chang family serves Mandarin and Szechuan food. "Mandarin is northern Chinese cooking," explains Robert. "It is cooked in a wok. It's not so much spicy as tasty, using a lot of black bean sauce and bean paste." Szechuan cooking is likewise prepared in a wok. "However, it comes from the west and is very spicy. The shrimp dish is Mandarin, the beef Szechuan." (To round out his picture of Chinese cuisine, Robert characterized the southern cuisine, Cantonese, as being on the sweet side, using much sweet-and-sour, and the eastern cuisine, Shang-Hai, as being steamed, not stir-fried, and featuring many cold appetizers.)

The restaurant's proprietor, Chuen Look Chang, grew up in Mandarin-style Peking, where he learned to cook at sixteen. He has not learned English and consequently, as Robert relates, the restaurant has stiff hiring requirements. "Waiters must not only speak Chinese, so my father can understand them, they must speak Mandarin as well."

In other ways, however, Mr. Chang has proven very adaptable. "We have Americanized our dishes a little bit, otherwise they wouldn't sell. For instance, in Hong-Kong Chinese food is served dry, not with a sauce. Here, Americans like sauce, so our food is much juicier. You might say we've used American ingenuity, Chinese-style."

7531 Wornall

CRAB RANGOON

1 pound cream cheese
½ pound crab meat
3 tablespoons garlic powder
2 tablespoons salt
2 tablespoons onion powder
2 tablespoons white wine
1 tablespoon sesame oil
10 wonton skins
½ cup Chinese hot mustard
½ cup Chinese sweet sauce

1. Mix together the cream cheese, crab meat, garlic powder, salt, onion powder, white wine and sesame oil.
2. Place about 2 tablespoons of the stuffing in the middle of the bottom half of each wonton. Fold the top half over onto the bottom. Seal by pinching together.
3. Deep-fry the wontons in 350° oil until golden brown. Serve with hot mustard and sweet sauce.

This recipe gives more stuffing than is needed for ten wontons. It freezes well and can be used again. The condiments are available at many American grocery stores and at all Chinese groceries.

SEAFOOD HOT AND SOUR SOUP

¼ pound crab meat
¼ pound shrimp, peeled and sliced in half
¼ pound scallops
8 snow peas, cut in half
8 black mushrooms, soaked and cut in slices
8 slices bean curd (tofu)
6 cups chicken stock
2 tablespoons cooking wine
3 tablespoons soy sauce
1 tablespoon salt
3 tablespoons vinegar
2 tablespoons hot pepper oil
1 tablespoon white pepper
1 tablespoon cornstarch dissolved in 2 tablespoons water
1 egg
1 tablespoon chopped green onion

1. Put the seafood, vegetables and bean curd in boiling stock. Simmer 5 minutes.
2. Add the wine, soy sauce, salt, vinegar, pepper oil, white pepper and cornstarch solution. Cook until the soup thickens. Beat egg with a fork and pour into the stock. Stir well. Just before serving, add the green onion.

Note: For the chicken stock you may dissolve 6 chicken bouillon cubes in 6 cups of hot water.

This soup is served all year 'round. It is probably the most popular homemade soup in China. It is usually made with pork, instead of seafood, but Americans like seafood much more than pork—a good example of our adapting Chinese cuisine to American tastes.

SHRIMP AND BROCCOLI WITH WINE SAUCE

16 medium shrimp, shelled and cleaned
3 egg whites, lightly beaten
2 tablespoons cornstarch
3 broccoli stems cut into 1½" florets
2 to 3 cups oil
1 tablespoon vinegar
1 tablespoon chopped garlic
1 tablespoon chopped green onion
3 tablespoons sherry
3 tablespoons sugar
½ tablespoon salt
Dash of flavor enhancer (optional)
1 tablespoon cornstarch dissolved in 2
   tablespoons water
½ teaspoon white pepper
Dash of sesame oil

1. Mix the shrimp with the egg whites and cornstarch.
2. Stir-fry the shrimp with the broccoli in a wok with hot oil for about 4 to 5 minutes over a fairly low heat (200° to 250°). Enough oil should be in the wok to cover the shrimp.
3. Remove the shrimp and broccoli and pour off all but 1 tablespoon of the oil. Return the shrimp and broccoli to the wok and add the remaining ingredients. Stir-fry until hot.

Mixing the shrimp with the egg whites tenderizes the shrimp. In preparing the dish, be careful that the oil does not get too hot. If it does, the shrimp will become crisp—something you don't want.

SZECHUAN SPICED SHREDDED BEEF

In China the dish is called "fish-flavored beef" because when it cools off it has a fishy taste.

1 pound flank steak, shredded
2 egg whites, lightly beaten
1 tablespoon cornstarch
3 to 4 cups oil
3 tablespoons hot pepper oil
½ tablespoon chopped ginger
½ tablespoon chopped garlic
½ tablespoon chopped green onion
1 tablespoon soybean paste
8 black mushrooms, soaked in cold water
   and shredded
4 ounces bamboo shoots, shredded
2 tablespoons soy sauce
1 tablespoon salt
1 tablespoon sugar
1 tablespoon sherry
Dash of vinegar and flavor enhancer (optional)

1. Mix the shredded beef with egg whites and the cornstarch. Stir-fry the beef in hot oil until it changes color. Enough oil should be in the wok to cover the beef.
2. Remove the beef and pour off the oil. Heat the hot pepper oil in the wok and add the ginger, garlic, green onion, soybean paste, mushrooms and bamboo shoots. Mix in the remaining ingredients and the beef. Cook over a high heat (400°) and serve.

Note: It will be much easier to shred the beef if you partially freeze it before shredding.

TOFFEE PINEAPPLE

1 egg
1 cup flour
½ cup cornstarch
2 cups water
16 pineapple chunks
8 to 10 cups oil
½ cup sugar
1 tablespoon sesame seeds

1. Combine egg, flour, cornstarch and water to make a batter. Mix the pineapple well with the batter.
2. Heat the oil in the wok to at least 350° (preferably 400°) and fry the pineapple 4 to 5 minutes or until light brown.
3. Pour off the oil and drain the pineapple. While the wok is still hot, melt the sugar in it until it "spins" or turns golden brown. Immediately add sesame seeds and the pineapple. Toss to cover the fruit with sugar and seeds.
4. Serve immediately after tossing by dipping each pineapple chunk into a bowl of cold water which will make each piece crispy on the outside and cool enough to eat.

For this recipe you can use practically any fruit that is large enough, such as apples, strawberries or bananas—but pineapple works the best. It is a little sour and juicy, and the sweet toffee coating combined with the sour pineapple gives a sweet-and-sour taste. Also, the crunchy outside goes well with the juicy inside.

A Restaurant

Dinner for Six

Iman Byaldi

Moules Marinière

Parchment Chicken

Wonton Salad

Praline Cheesecake

Wines:

With Iman Byaldi—Gewürztraminer
With Moules—Chardonnay
With Chicken—Vouvray
With Cheesecake—Brut Champagne

Don Anderson, Proprietor

The Prospect of Westport is a place that transports you for a moment in time to some other place, whether remembered, imagined, or simply enjoyed. Owner-operator Don Anderson is the man responsible for the existence not only of the Prospect but also for Westport Square, a renovated mid-town oasis of retail and entertainment establishments amid courtyards and arcades.

The Prospect seats 125 in an ample space, the focal point of which is an atrium rising two stories skyward, providing light for the profusion of plants and space for the resounding classical music. Natural materials and fresh foods reflect an honesty and sensibility that attract a discriminating and creative clientele. Much of the tile, glass, fabric and brass were acquired in Europe by the architect and the owner, both of whom are Anglophiles.

The sense of freshness, airiness and vitality that characterizes the environment also describes the food. A totally à la carte menu offers an eclectic selection of tastes, as the menu says, "to be enjoyed any time of day or evening in sizes and combinations to please your hunger, your mood, your spirit." The menu allows for adventure and experimentation.

"Quality, taste and beautiful presentation are my major concerns," says Bonnie Winston, food and design consultant, who created the menu and the operating philosophy of the restaurant. These elements combined with intelligent service and a beautiful environment make the Prospect a delightful place to dine.

4109 Pennsylvania

IMAN BYALDI

A classic Middle Eastern dish, its name is translated "... and the priest fainted"—because it was so good, of course!

3 small eggplants
Olive or vegetable oil
1 medium onion, chopped
1 teaspoon finely minced garlic
3 tomatoes, seeded and diced
1 cup coarsely chopped pitted black olives
1 cup dried currants, plumped in hot water
1 tablespoon curry powder
1 tablespoon **Garam Masala** (see next page)
1 teaspoon celery salt
1½ teaspoons thyme
Salt and pepper to taste
Lemon juice to taste
Pignolia or pine nuts, lightly sautéed in butter
Parsley

1. Peel eggplants. Halve lengthwise and chop into small cubes.
2. Cover bottom of large frying pan with oil and sauté onion, garlic and eggplant just until tender.
3. Mix remaining ingredients except nuts and parsley and remove from heat immediately.
4. Taste for seasoning, adding salt, pepper and/or lemon juice if desired. Refrigerate.
5. Serve as a spread, generously heaped in a beautiful serving bowl or presented in halved eggplant shells à la Mother Nature, garnished with pine nuts and parsley. Lavash or some similar cracker accompanies well.

Note: Equally delicious served cold, tossed with chilled noodles as a salad, or hot, over noodles or spaghetti squash as an entrée item.

Garam Masala

This spice mixture may also be found at some Asian or Indian markets.

25 cardamom pods (seeds only)
½ cup whole peppercorns
⅓ cup whole cumin seeds
¼ cup whole coriander seeds
3 (3") sticks cinnamon
4 to 6 whole cloves

Combine ingredients and grind very fine using a blender or coffee grinder.

MOULES MARINIERE
MUSSELS STEAMED IN WINE AND HERBS

Serve with lots of French bread and butter.

5 pounds mussels
1½ cups chopped onion
2 tablespoons finely minced garlic
¾ cup chopped parsley
2 tablespoons oregano
1 tablespoon basil
1 tablespoon thyme
1 teaspoon salt
1 bay leaf
1 to 2 small dried red peppers
½ pound butter
2 cups dry white wine

1. Scrub mussels well. Remove beards. Let soak in cold water 1 to 2 hours. (A small quantity of salt or baking soda can be added to the water to purge the mussels.)
2. Combine onion, garlic, ½ cup parsley, oregano, basil, thyme, salt, bay leaf, peppers, butter and wine; bring to a boil.
3. Add mussels, cover tightly and steam about 5 minutes, until mussels open. Any unopened mussels should be discarded.
4. Remove mussels to bowls and pour cooking liquor over. Garnish with remaining parsley.

Note: The mussels might also be presented at table in the cooking vessel, with a ladle to serve.

PARCHMENT CHICKEN

This method of cooking is referred to as en papillote, *a classic technique that allows the contents to obtain their optimum moisture and flavor.*

3 large chicken breasts, skinned, boned and
    halved
6 Chinese sausages (Lop Cheung)
Parchment paper
6 large mushrooms, thickly sliced
6 tablespoons thinly sliced scallions (white
    and green parts)
Marinade (see next page)

1. Marinate chicken breasts at least 1 hour.
2. Steam Chinese sausage 15 minutes. Slice about ¼" thick on a deep diagonal.
3. Preheat oven to 350°.
4. For each serving, cut parchment paper into a heart shape large enough to enclose chicken breast with a 2" to 3" border.
5. Place each halved chicken breast on right half of opened parchment paper heart. Cover with 6 slices of Chinese sausage, then with 6 overlapping mushroom slices. Sprinkle lightly with scallions.
6. Fold left half of heart over right so edges line up. Crimp outside edge all around by folding edge over itself as you go, ending by lightly twisting bottom point. Each packet must be completely and tightly sealed in order to retain steam and cook properly. (Packets may be prepared ahead and refrigerated at this point until ready to cook.)
7. Place packets on baking sheet and bake in preheated oven for 15 minutes or microwave 2 minutes for each packet.
8. Serve in packets, allowing each guest to gently tear open.

Parchment paper is available in most gourmet kitchen shops. Aluminum foil will do in a pinch (but do not use in microwave oven).

Marinade

½ cup Japanese soy sauce
½ cup dry sherry
½ cup Hoisin sauce
2½ tablespoons cornstarch
3 tablespoons sesame oil
1½ tablespoons sugar
¼ teaspoon pepper

Combine ingredients.

WONTON SALAD

This is a salad to entice all the senses. It is substantial enough to be served as an entrée also.

24 wonton skins, cut into ½" strips
1 large or 2 small heads iceberg lettuce
8 ounces mung bean sprouts
¼ cup chopped parsley or watercress sprigs
8 ounces water chestnuts, thinly sliced
½ pound cooked chicken, shredded
¼ pound ham, finely julienned
Sesame Dressing

1. Fry wonton strips in hot oil until golden. Drain on paper towels and salt lightly.
2. Shred lettuce and mound in large bowl or platter.
3. Cover with bean sprouts, sprinkle with parsley (or watercress) and distribute water chestnuts over evenly.
4. Mound chicken in center of salad. Make a small well in center of chicken and fill with ham.
5. Arrange fried wonton around outer perimeter of salad, thereby creating concentric circles of taste, texture and color.
6. Toss at table with **Sesame Dressing** or offer dressing to spoon over individual portions.

Sesame Dressing

$1/_3$ cup white vinegar
$1/_3$ cup sesame seeds
$1/_3$ cup soy sauce
3 tablespoons sugar
¾ teaspoon finely minced fresh ginger root
¾ teaspoon finely minced garlic
½ teaspoon Worcestershire sauce
1 teaspoon dry mustard
$1/_3$ teaspoon salt
1½ tablespoons thinly sliced scallions
3 tablespoons sesame oil
$2/_3$ cup vegetable oil

Combine all ingredients; mix well.

PRALINE CHEESECAKE

Crust

1¼ cups graham cracker crumbs
¼ cup sugar
¼ cup pecans, lightly toasted in oven and
    finely chopped, not ground
¼ cup melted sweet butter

1. Preheat oven to 300°.
2. Combine ingredients in a bowl, mixing thoroughly.
3. Press into bottom and sides of a 9" to 10" springform pan. Bake
   10 minutes in preheated oven.

Filling

1½ pounds cream cheese, softened
1 cup brown sugar
1 (5⅓-ounce) can evaporated milk
2 tablespoons flour
1½ teaspoons vanilla
3 large eggs

1. Preheat oven to 325°.
2. Cream cheese and sugar well in mixer.
3. Add evaporated milk, flour and vanilla, mix well.
4. Add eggs 1 at a time, mixing well after each addition.
5. Pour into crust. Bake in preheated oven for 50 minutes.

This rich confection is still more appealing when topped with pecans and maple syrup.

SAVOY GRILL

Dinner for Six

Crab Meat Ravigote

Artichoke Hearts Mimosa

Lobster Thermidor

Mocha Coconut Pie

Wines:
With Crab Meat and Artichokes—Vouvray
With Lobster Thermidor—Pouilly-Fuissé

Don Lee, Owner and General Manager
Andy Brandolese, Executive Chef

By all rights, the Savoy Grill ought to stand on the corner of 12th Street and Vine, the most famous of Kansas City intersections. Residing instead at the corner of 9th and Central since the turn of the century, the Savoy is the matriarch of the city's restaurants, incomparably capturing the flavor and atmosphere of a midwestern city.

Western murals line the walls. Stained-glass windows filter in soft light. A high, beamed ceiling, stained oak paneling, leather booths and brass lanterns give the dining room a spacious, nineteenth-century restaurant saloon effect. In fact, the restaurant and the building that houses it were accepted in 1974 into the National Register of Historic Places.

True to its western ambiance, the restaurant serves highly regarded steaks. Proprietor of the Savoy for twenty-one years, Don Lee proudly claims that his is the only restaurant in town that dry ages its prime meat: "Everyone is now buying what is called 'box-beef', beef that is vacuum packed and that doesn't shrink in a refrigerator. Dry aging meat in a refrigerator causes shrinkage and is thus uneconomical, but flavor is enhanced."

While Lee boasts about the quality of his meat, the Savoy's pride and joy are lobster and other seafood items. The kitchen contains its own lobster tank, and the restaurant offers the most extensive selection of seafood dishes in town. Either way, steak or seafood, you can't miss at the Savoy.

9th and Central

CRAB MEAT RAVIGOTE

4½ cups lump crab meat
1 cup **Ravigote Sauce**
1 head of lettuce, shredded
2 to 3 tomatoes, depending on size, cut into wedges

1. Blend the crab meat with the **Ravigote Sauce,** being careful not to break up the crab meat.
2. Chill in the refrigerator and serve on a bed of shredded lettuce with tomato wedges.

Ravigote Sauce

This recipe makes 1¼ cups.

1 cup mayonnaise
1½ tablespoons minced bell pepper
1½ tablespoons minced green onions
1½ tablespoons minced anchovies
1½ tablespoons minced pimientos

Mix all ingredients together and chill.

Note: The Ravigote Sauce should be prepared at least 8 hours ahead of serving. The key ingredient is the anchovies and they must sit in the mayonnaise for some time to give it their flavor. Prepared mayonnaise is fine here, but do use whole anchovies rather than anchovy paste.

ARTICHOKE HEARTS MIMOSA

18 canned artichoke hearts, drained
1 head of lettuce
1 tablespoon chopped pimiento
3 hard-cooked eggs, chopped
2 to 3 tomatoes, depending on size, cut into
   wedges
Oil and Vinegar Dressing

1. On each of 6 salad plates, arrange 3 artichoke hearts on a bed of
   lettuce.
2. Sprinkle on pimiento and eggs.
3. Serve with tomato wedges and **Oil and Vinegar Dressing**.

Oil and Vinegar Dressing

1 cup olive oil
⅓ cup vinegar
½ teaspoon dry mustard
1 tablespoon chopped parsley
½ teaspoon tarragon
½ teaspoon chervil
½ clove shallot, chopped
½ clove garlic, finely minced
Salt and white pepper to taste

Combine all ingredients and mix well. Shake well before serving.

Note: The dressing for the salad should be prepared a day ahead so the herbs will impart their flavor to the oil and vinegar.

LOBSTER THERMIDOR

6 (1-pound) lobsters
¼ pound butter
1 cup flour
4 cups milk
¼ bunch green onions, chopped
¼ bunch parsley, chopped
1 large shallot, finely chopped
½ cup coarsely chopped mushrooms
½ teaspoon dry mustard
Salt to taste
½ teaspoon white pepper
½ cup grated Parmesan cheese
¼ cup sherry

1. Boil lobsters approximately 15 minutes in a large kettle of salted water.
2. Let them cool, then split in half and remove the lobster meat. Cut meat in large chunks.
3. Melt butter in a saucepan. Add flour, stirring over low heat for 2 minutes. Remove from heat and pour in the milk. Stir well to mix with flour and butter. Return sauce to heat and bring to boil. Remove from heat.
4. Add remaining ingredients to the sauce, reserving 2 tablespoons Parmesan.
5. Mix well, then add the chopped lobster meat.
6. Preheat oven to 250°.
7. Stuff lobster shells and dust with remaining Parmesan cheese.
8. Bake for 10 minutes in preheated oven.

Note: The sauce for Lobster Thermidor has to be thick because it must stay in the shell. If the sauce is too thin when it is heated, it will run. It should be sharp tasting and heavy enough to stand on your finger.

MOCHA COCONUT PIE

The only thing I don't like about this recipe is that it is super rich, full of calories. Obviously, I wouldn't serve it to diet-conscious guests. The whipped cream topping is mainly for appearance, but light cream goes well with a heavy pie.

1¼ cups canned sweet shredded coconut
2 ounces unsweetened chocolate
2 tablespoons brandy
2 tablespoons instant coffee powder
½ pound unsalted butter, softened
½ cup sugar
2 large eggs
½ cup ground hazelnuts
½ cup ground blanched almonds
1 cup heavy cream, whipped and sweetened with 2 tablespoons sugar

1. Line the bottom and sides of an 8" pie plate with shredded coconut and bake in a 250° oven for 1 hour or until golden.
2. Transfer the pie plate to a rack and let the shell cool.
3. In the top of a double boiler set over hot water, melt unsweetened chocolate with brandy and instant coffee.
4. Cream together unsalted butter and sugar. Beat in eggs, 1 at a time, beating well after each addition.
5. Add the chocolate mixture, hazelnuts and almonds.
6. Transfer the filling to the shell and chill the pie for at least 3 hours.
7. Serve each slice with a dab of whipped cream.

The Old Apple Farm

Dinner for Six

Potato Soup

Marshmallow Salad

Baked Chicken 'n' Butter and Cream

Green Rice

Bran Muffins

Frozen Lemon Dessert

Wine:
With Chicken—Mouton-Cadet Blanc

Les and Lloyd Stephenson, Owners
Charlie Myers, Chef

"Go east, diners of Kansas City. Go east." This must have been the slogan of Les and Lloyd Stephenson in the early years of their thirty-four-year-old restaurant. Located practically in Independence, well east of downtown Kansas City, the twin brothers felt they had to create a special restaurant to lure the hungry so far away from their homes.

"We have a terrible location," declares Lloyd. "There was no local business when we opened so we had to survive on town traffic. The only way, as I saw it, to get people to drive this far was to have something outstanding. The food had to be different and had to have value." In keeping with their semi-rural setting, they devised a country menu with several hickory-smoked items, oven-fresh rolls and fried fritters. Inside, they created a barn-like setting with the walls of the several dining rooms painted red and waitresses in country dresses.

In particular, the Stephensons oriented their restaurant to please women. "The woman decides where to go eat," says Lloyd. "She's got to like it. We've got to romance the women." To that end the brothers designed one of the first atmosphere restaurants in town.

The success of their first restaurant has prompted the twins to open two more, one near Kansas City International Airport, the other in Jane, Missouri, near Bella Vista, Arkansas. Now Kansas City diners who want to sample some good ol' country cooking can go east, or they can go north, or they can go south—it doesn't matter to the twins.

40 Highway and Lee's Summit Road

POTATO SOUP

6 medium potatoes, peeled and diced
2 tablespoons butter
1 medium carrot, diced
¼ cup finely chopped onion
2 tablespoons flour
1 quart milk
2 tablespoons finely chopped parsley
1 tablespoon salt
½ teaspoon seasoning salt
¼ teaspoon Accent
¼ teaspoon red pepper
1 chicken bouillon cube

1. Cook potatoes in boiling salted water until tender. Drain.
2. Melt butter in 3-quart kettle until golden brown. Add carrot and onion. Cover and cook until tender. Remove from heat.
3. Blend flour into butter and vegetables. Stir in milk, making sure to mix well.
4. Add half of the potatoes. Mash the other half of the potatoes and add with the remaining ingredients. Heat until steaming hot.

After people drive a long way out here, this soup warms them up.

MARSHMALLOW SALAD

1 (30-ounce) can pineapple chunks
2 eggs, beaten
3 tablespoons cider vinegar
2 tablespoons flour
1 cup whipping cream
1 tablespoon powdered sugar
½ pound large marshmallows, quartered

1. Drain pineapple, measuring ½ cup syrup into the top of a double boiler. Save the drained pineapple (2½ cups).
2. Add eggs, vinegar and flour to the syrup and mix well. Stir over hot water until thick. Cool.
3. Beat cream until stiff. Beat in sugar.
4. Fold the cream into the cooled egg mixture. Fold in the pineapple and marshmallows. Chill overnight.

The thing you have to remember about this recipe is to chill the salad overnight. Doing so lets you make it a day before and also the marshmallows acquire some of the pineapple taste.

BAKED CHICKEN 'N' BUTTER AND CREAM

2 cut-up frying chickens
1 cup flour
1 tablespoon salt
1 teaspoon paprika
½ teaspoon pepper
¼ pound butter
3 cups milk

1. Dip chicken pieces into water. Coat with mixture of flour and seasonings.
2. Put skin side up into 2 (13"x 9"x 2") baking pans. Dot with butter. Bake at 425° for 30 minutes, or until golden brown. Remove from oven.
3. Pour milk around chicken. Cover with aluminum foil. Return to oven and bake at 350° for 45 minutes.

The nice thing about this chicken recipe is that because it is a two-step preparation you can do part of it ahead. Even a day ahead you could do the first baking of the chicken and do the second baking right before serving to ensure freshness.

GREEN RICE

2½ cups cooked rice
¾ cup chopped parsley
⅓ cup grated Cheddar cheese
¼ cup chopped onion
3 tablespoons chopped green pepper
1 small clove garlic, minced
12 ounces evaporated milk
2 small eggs, beaten
⅓ cup vegetable oil
2 teaspoons salt
¼ teaspoon seasoning salt
¼ teaspoon pepper
¼ teaspoon Accent
Juice and grated rind of ½ lemon
Paprika

1. Mix rice, parsley, cheese, onion, green pepper and garlic in a greased 2-quart casserole. Blend in the remaining ingredients. Sprinkle with paprika.
2. Bake at 350° about 45 minutes or until the consistency of a soft custard.

We picked this recipe out of the Kansas City Star. We'll get our recipes anywhere so long as they fit our menu. This is a little different, and we try not to do the same things that the housewife makes herself.

BRAN MUFFINS

This recipe makes 12 (3-inch) muffins.

½ cup 100% All Bran
½ cup Raisin Bran
¼ cup raisins
1 cup milk
2 tablespoons shortening
¼ cup sugar
1 egg
1 cup sifted flour
1 teaspoon baking powder
½ teaspoon salt

1. Soak cereals and raisins in milk for 5 minutes.
2. Cream shortening and sugar. Beat in egg until smooth.
3. Sift together flour, baking powder and salt. Stir into shortening mixture alternately with cereal mixture, just until blended. Do not overmix.
4. Fill greased muffin cups two-thirds full. Bake at 400° for 25 to 30 minutes.

These muffins are very quick. There's no rising, no stirring. They require one-step baking.

FROZEN LEMON DESSERT

½ cup graham cracker crumbs
¾ cup sugar
2 tablespoons butter, melted
2 eggs, separated
1 egg, whole
2 to 3 tablespoons grated lemon rind
¼ cup lemon juice
¼ teaspoon cream of tartar
1 cup whipping cream
1 tablespoon powdered sugar
$^1/_8$ teaspoon vanilla

1. Mix together graham cracker crumbs, ¼ cup sugar and butter. Press mixture firmly into bottom of 10" x 6" x 2" pan. Chill.
2. Beat egg yolks and whole egg in medium-sized saucepan. Stir in ¼ cup sugar, lemon rind and juice. Stir over low heat until thick. Cool.
3. Beat egg whites until foamy. Add cream of tartar and continue beating. Beat in remaining sugar, a tablespoon at a time, until stiff peaks form.
4. Beat cream until stiff. Beat in powdered sugar and vanilla. Fold the whipped cream into the egg whites.
5. Fold the cooled lemon mixture into the cream and egg white mixture. Pour into crust. Freeze.

This dessert is very light; good after a heavy meal. It holds well in the freezer for weeks, so a hostess can make it ahead of serving.

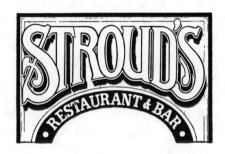

Dinner for Six

Chicken Noodle Soup

Chicken-Fried Steak

Cottage Fries

Biscuits

Brandy Ice

Wine:
Mouton-Cadet Blanc

James Hogan and Michael Donegan, Owners
Larry Hunt, Kitchen Manager

Often a restaurant's décor can contribute almost as much to the enjoyment of a fine meal as the food itself. Some establishments forget that without the food element the décor becomes an unnecessary pretext. Happily, Stroud's combines both with fantastic results.

At very reasonable prices, the dinner menu offers a large selection of pan-fried chicken ("The best in the world," say the owners modestly), barbequed ribs, Kansas City strip steaks and pan-fried catfish, all served in large portions with soup or salad and potatoes of your choice with pan-fried gravy. The homemade cinnamon rolls are truly a taste treat.

The owners, Jim Hogan and Mike Donegan, have tastefully and successfully combined their love for antiques and the antiquated in a setting which makes for a truly different dining experience. The building itself is not exactly Early American or even Victorian. If your table is listing to port or starboard, it is not due to the improper adjustments of its legs: it is probably one of the Stroud's treasures. The antiques, some valuable and some not, are very tastefully placed on the walls, behind the bar, and hanging from the ceiling. If the paraphernalia doesn't fascinate you, just relax at the table and enjoy Helen Bess's piano, and perhaps join in the sing-along of America's old tunes.

The treasures may not be antiques, the building may not be Victorian, the playing and singing may not be like an evening at the "Met," but the food and the drinks are worth any wait you may have. If you are a visitor to Kansas City, you should not leave town without visiting Stroud's. The people back home won't believe you when you tell them about it.

1015 East 85th Street

CHICKEN NOODLE SOUP

3 quarts salted water
3 chicken breasts
2 tablespoons chicken soup base (bouillon
   cubes can be substituted)
Pinch of oregano
Salt and pepper to taste
1 (12-ounce) package Reames egg noodles
1 stalk celery, chopped

1. Bring salted water to boil.
2. Drop in chicken breasts. Add soup base, oregano and salt and
   pepper to taste. Boil for 1 hour. Remove chicken breasts and set
   aside.
3. Add noodles and chopped celery. Bring to boil again and simmer
   for 30 minutes.
4. De-bone chicken breasts and dice the meat.
5. Add meat to stock and serve.

*Mr. Hunt makes his noodles from scratch but has found frozen
Reames egg noodles to be a very good substitute.*

CHICKEN-FRIED STEAK

Salt and pepper
1 tablespoon paprika
2 cups flour
1 egg
4 cups milk
6 (5- to 6-ounce) cubed steaks
Gravy

1. Add salt, pepper and paprika to the flour.
2. Beat the egg and mix with milk to make a batter.
3. Dredge each steak thoroughly in seasoned flour and then dip into the batter of milk and egg.
4. Dredge each steak again in flour and pound out with a meat mallet to tenderize. This breaks down any coarse meat tissues.
5. Heat a well-greased griddle or heavy skillet until hot but not smoking. Add steaks and cook until golden brown on both sides.
6. To serve, pour **Gravy** over steaks.

Gravy

Cracklings of **Chicken-Fried Steak**
6 tablespoons flour
3 cups milk
Salt and pepper to taste

1. Cover the bottom ½" of a medium-sized frying pan with the cracklings and grease left from the fried meat.
2. Spoon in flour and stir until it has the appearance of paste.
3. Bring to a boil. Slowly add milk.
4. Cook slowly until the gravy returns to a boil, stirring constantly to keep the gravy from sticking to bottom of the pan. Season to taste.

A whisk is very helpful for blending the milk into the flour and drippings. Stirring with the whisk prevents lumps from forming.

COTTAGE FRIES

8 large Idaho potatoes
Salt and pepper

1. Preheat deep-fat fryer to 360°.
2. Peel and slice the potatoes lengthwise. Pat dry on paper towels.
3. Drop the potatoes into preheated deep-fat fryer and cook until crisp and golden brown.
4. Pat off grease; add salt and pepper to taste.

What makes these special is using Idaho potatoes instead of red potatoes. Try leaving the skins on for a new twist.

BISCUITS

This recipe makes 12 biscuits.

2 cups flour
3 teaspoons baking powder
1 teaspoon salt
¼ cup cold shortening (such as Crisco)
¾ cup cold milk

1. Preheat oven to 450°.
2. Combine dry ingredients in a bowl. Cut in shortening with a pastry blender.
3. Add cold milk and stir until the batter cleans the sides of the bowl and the dough forms a ball.
4. Pat out ½" thick and cut with biscuit cutter. Place close together on a greased baking sheet.
5. Bake in preheated oven for 12 minutes.

Note: If you prefer a crisp biscuit, do not place them close together and they will brown on all sides.

BRANDY ICE

The trick to this dessert is to keep your guests from having too many seconds.

6 scoops vanilla ice cream
¾ cup brandy
¾ cup dark crème de cacao
Nutmeg

1. Place ice cream, brandy and crème de cacao in a blender. Blend until the mixture has the consistency of a thick malt.
2. Serve in large champagne glasses with a pinch of nutmeg on top.

TASSO'S

Dinner for Four

Avgolemono

Greek Salad

Kotopoulo Reganato

Cretekia Patoutha

Wine:
With Chicken—Cambas Demestica

Tasso Kalliris, Owner
Katina Kalliris, Chef

Tasso's is a Greek island in the middle of Kansas City. In his narrow, one-room restaurant, Tasso Kalliris has transplanted a bit of Corinth, Greece, his original hometown, to western Missouri. Tapes of festive Greek music play night and day, and on weekend nights Greek dancers entertain diners. The restaurant jumps with a vitality so pleasing to Tasso that he can't imagine changing a thing. "The restaurant has to stay as it is," Tasso declares. "My customers wouldn't want anything different."

While the music may make you want to dance, Tasso's food will keep you in your seat. "I serve true Greek food," he proudly claims. "The correct Greek food is in Athens, and Corinth is close to Athens. In fact, Corinthian food is the best in Greece."

Tasso's menu offers sandwiches and salads for the timid and more sumptuous complete dinners for the ravenous. Like a highly seasoned litany, oregano, lemon and garlic appear throughout the cooking. "Greek food is not mild," Tasso remarks. "It has a lot of flavor."

211 West 75th Street

AVGOLEMONO

1 (3-pound) chicken, quartered (with giblets,
   back and neck reserved)
1 onion, chopped
1 stalk celery, chopped
1 teaspoon basil
1 teaspoon oregano
½ cup uncooked rice
2 eggs, beaten
Juice of 6 to 7 lemons
4 teaspoons olive oil
Salt and pepper

1. Simmer the chicken (including giblets, back and neck), onion, celery
   and herbs in 2 quarts of water for 2 to 3 hours. Strain broth, reserving
   chicken. (You will need 5 cups of broth. If you have too much,
   reduce over heat; if you have too little, add enough water to make
   5 cups.) Cut chicken meat into bite-size pieces. Set aside.
2. Twenty minutes before serving, bring broth to a boil and add the
   rice. Cover, return to a boil, then reduce heat and simmer for 20
   minutes.
3. Just before serving, add the chicken, beaten eggs, lemon juice and
   olive oil. Stir until eggs are cooked. Salt and pepper to taste. Serve hot.

*This is the most typical of Greek soups. The sharpness of the lemon juice
stimulates the appetite.*

GREEK SALAD

1 head iceberg lettuce, cleaned, trimmed and cut into bite-size pieces
1 cucumber, peeled and cut into chunks
½ medium onion, sliced into rings
2 small tomatoes, cut into wedges
20 Greek olives
½ cup feta cheese
1 teaspoon oregano
Greek Dressing

Place lettuce on salad plates and attractively arrange cucumber, onion, tomatoes, olives and feta cheese over the lettuce. Sprinkle oregano over each salad. Dress with **Greek Dressing**.

Greek Dressing

⅔ cup olive oil
Juice of 2 lemons
1 tablespoon white vinegar (or more if you
   like a tart dressing)
1 teaspoon oregano
Salt and pepper to taste

Mix all ingredients well.

The feta cheese and Greek olives are what make this salad distinctive. The dressing should be fairly tart.

KOTOPOULO REGANATO

2 (3-pound) chickens, quartered
2 cups salted water
⅓ cup olive oil
Juice of 2 lemons
4 tablespoons oregano
1 tablespoon salt
1 tablespoon black pepper
2 cloves garlic, minced

1. Rinse the chicken in water. Place in salted water and soak for 10 minutes. Rinse again.
2. Prepare a marinade by combining olive oil, lemon juice, oregano,

salt and pepper. Pour marinade around the chicken in a baking pan. Let the chicken marinate for at least 2 hours, preferably longer.
3. When ready to cook, sprinkle minced garlic on top of the chicken. Cover the baking pan with foil and bake the chicken in a 300° oven for 2 hours.
4. Ten minutes or so before serving, uncover the chicken so it will color a little.

The chicken should be quite tasty, quite highly seasoned.

CRETEKIA PATOUTHA

¾ cup olive oil
½ cup water
Juice of 1 lemon
½ teaspoon salt
¼ cup sugar
1½ cups flour, sifted
½ teaspoon baking powder
1 cup ground pistachios or walnuts
1 cup ground almonds
1 cup sesame seeds
1 cup honey
1 egg, beaten

1. Mix together the oil, water, lemon juice, salt and sugar in a bowl. Add flour and baking powder, mixing well. Work into a smooth dough.
2. Roll dough out on a floured board to a thickness of ¼". Cut into 2" squares.
3. In a separate bowl, mix together the ground nuts, sesame seeds and honey. Place 1 to 2 tablespoons of the filling in the center of each square. Moisten the edges and fold over the filling. Press together and pinch firmly to close. Brush with beaten egg.
4. Bake at 325° for 15 minutes or until golden. Serve warm or cool.

Greek pastries, like this one, are usually eaten between meals in Greece, rather than as a dessert which usually consists of fruit. In America, the pastries go fine as desserts.

Appetizers

Champignons Magiques (Plaza III)	129
Crab Meat Ravigote (Savoy)	157
Crab Rangoon (Princess Gardens)	139
Deep-Fried Artichoke Hearts (Costello's)	49
Escargots Gourmands (La Méditérranée)	113
Fresh Red Apple Relish (Dinner Horn)	57
Homos (Al-Roubaie)	15
Iman Byaldi (Prospect)	147
Lobster Américaine (Alameda Plaza)	4 ˙
Moules Marinière (Prospect)	148
Mousse de Saumon aux Ecrevisses (La Bonne Auberge)	31
Mushrooms Escargot (Houlihan's)	79
Oysters Rockefeller (Harry Starker's)	70
Scaccia (Italian Gardens)	89
Tabouleh (Nabil's)	121
Tomatoes Sicilian (Jennie's)	107

Beverages

Café Calypso (Jasper's)	103
Greenhouse Forty-Three (Costello's)	53
Sammy Ciao (Italian Gardens)	95

Breads

Biscuits (Stroud's)	176
Bran Muffins (Stephenson's)	168
Camembert Beignets (Alameda Plaza)	10
Cheese Bread Sticks (Dinner Horn)	58
Garlic Toast (Jennie's)	108
Golden Pumpkin Muffins (Dinner Horn)	63
Pizza Dough (Italian Gardens)	90

Desserts and Dessert Accents

Almond Pastry Cups (La Bonne Auberge)	36
Bananas Foster Crêpes (Houlihan's)	84
Brandy Alexander Mousse (Jasper's)	102
Brandy Ice (Stroud's)	177
Camembert Beignets (Alameda Plaza)	10
Chocolate Mousse (Nabil's)	125
Chocolate Mousse Raphael (Alameda Plaza)	11

Crêpes (Houlihan's)   84
Cretekia Patoutha (Tasso's)   183
Dutch Strawberry Trifle (Dinner Horn)   64
Foster Sauce (Houlihan's)   85
Frozen Lemon Dessert (Stephenson's)   169
Génoise Circles (La Bonne Auberge)   36
Greenhouse Forty-Three (Costello's)   53
Mocha Coconut Pie (Savoy)   161
Mousse au Chocolat Blanc (La Méditérranée)   117
Lemon Ice (Jennie's)   109
Pecan Pie (Bristol)   44
Plaza III Cream (Plaza III)   135
Praline Cheesecake (Prospect)   152
Sammy Ciao (Italian Gardens)   95
Strawberries in Plaza III Cream (Plaza III)   134
Strawberries Romanoff (Al-Roubaie)   19
Sugarbush Mountain Maple Mousse (American)   26
Timbale Elysée (La Bonne Auberge)   35
Toffee Pineapple (Princess Garden)   143
Vanilla Cream Rum Sauce (American)   27
Vanilla Ice Cream (La Bonne Auberge)   37

Entrées

Baked Chicken n' Butter and Cream (Stephenson's)   166
Broiled Halibut (Bristol)   43
Chicken Breast Piquanti (Jennie's)   109
Chicken-Fried Steak (Stroud's)   174
Côtes de Veau aux Morilles (La Bonne Auberge)   33
Kotopoulo Reganato (Tasso's)   182
Lemon Veal with Eggplant (Jasper's)   101
Lobster Thermidor (Savoy)   160
Mignon de Veau Polignac (La Méditérranée)   115
Parchment Chicken (Prospect)   149
Peppered Duck with Figs in Red Port Sauce (American)   24
Roasted Crisp Duck (Houlihan's)   81
Saltimbocca alla Roma (Alameda Plaza)   7
Sautéed Breast of Chicken Kiev (Harry Starker's)   71
Seafood-Stuffed Zucchini (Costello's)   52
Shrimp and Broccoli with Wine Sauce (Princess Garden)   141
Stuffed Pork Chops with Apple Corn Bread Dressing
    (Dinner Horn)   60
Szechuan Spiced Shredded Beef (Princess Garden)   142
Turkish Lamb Kabob (Al-Roubaie)   17
Veal with Dijon (Nabil's)   124

Veal Potenza (Italian Gardens)   93
Veal Sauté Smitaine (Plaza III)   133

Pastas

Fettuccine all'Alfredo (Jasper's)   99
Linguine with White Clam Sauce (Jennie's)   108
Tortellini (Italian Gardens)   92

Salad Dressings

Creamy Anchovy Dressing (Alameda Plaza)   9
French Dressing (Houlihan's)   80
Greek Dressing (Tasso's)   182
Italian Salad Dressing (Jasper's)   100
Mint Vinaigrette Dressing (Nabil's)   123
Oil and Vinegar Dressing (Savoy)   159
Sesame Dressing (Prospect)   151
Vinaigrette (La Méditérranée)   114
Vinaigrette Dressing (Bristol)   42

Salads

Artichoke Hearts Mimosa (Savoy)   158
Bibb Lettuce and Spinach Salad (Alameda Plaza)   9
Boston Bibb Lettuce with Soy-Sesame Vinaigrette
  (American)   26
Boston Lettuce Salad (Houlihan's)   80
Greek Salad (Tasso's)   182
Marshmallow Salad (Stephenson's)   166
Romaine Salad with Mint Vinaigrette Dressing (Nabil's)   123
Salade de Saison (La Méditérranée)   114
Tomato, Onion and Anchovy Salad (Jasper's)   100
Tossed Salad with Blue Cheese Dressing (Costello's)   51
Vine-Ripe Tomato Slices Vinaigrette (Bristol)   42
Wonton Salad (Prospect)   150

Sauces and Special Seasonings

Apple Corn Bread Dressing (Dinner Horn)   60
Beurre Manié (Harry Starker's)   69
Cheddar Cheese Sauce (Plaza III)   130
Demi-Glace de Viande (La Méditérranée)   115
Escargot Butter (Houlihan's)   79

Figs in Red Port Sauce (American) 24
Garam Masala (Prospect) 148
Gravy (Stroud's) 174
Hollandaise Sauce (Harry Starker's) 74
Hollandaise Sauce (Plaza III) 132
Kiev Butter (Harry Starker's) 72
Kiev Sauce (Harry Starker's) 72
Lemon Butter (Costello's) 49
Marinade (Prospect) 150
Meat Sauce (Italian Gardens) 90
Mornay Sauce (Harry Starker's) 70
Ravigote Sauce (Savoy) 157
Sauce à l'Orange (Houlihan's) 82
Shrimp Sauce (La Bonne Auberge) 32
Tangy Raisin Sauce (Dinner Horn) 61

Sorbets

Lemon Sherbet with Kiwi (Alameda Plaza) 6
Sorbet au Champagne (La Bonne Auberge) 32

Soups

Al-Roubaie Soup (Al-Roubaie) 16
Avgolemono (Tasso's) 181
Bookbinder Soup (Harry Starker's) 69
Chicken Noodle Soup (Stroud's) 173
Chicken Soup with Tortellini (Italian Gardens) 91
Chilled Potage Singapore (Alameda Plaza) 3
Cream of Avocado Soup (Nabil's) 122
Crème de Celeri (La Méditérranée) 116
James Beard's Clam Soup That Cures (American) 23
Potato Soup (Stephenson's) 165
Seafood Hot and Sour Soup (Princess Garden) 140
Spring Broccoli Soup (Dinner Horn) 59
Steak Soup (Plaza III) 131
Wedding Soup (Costello's) 50

Vegetables and Side Dishes

Artichoke Florentine (Alameda Plaza) 8
Broccoli in Hollandaise Sauce (Plaza III) 132
Cauliflower (Houlihan's) 83
Cottage Fries (Stroud's) 175

Ginger-Glazed Carrots (Dinner Horn)   61
Green Corn Pudding (Dinner Horn)   62
Green Rice (Stephenson's)   167
Italian Spinach (Italian Gardens)   94
Medley of Garden Vegetables (Harry Starker's)   74
Miniature Meatballs (Costello's)   50
Potatoes Al-Roubaie (Al-Roubaie)   18
Straw Potatoes (Alameda Plaza)   5
Sugar Snap Peas (American)   25
Twice-Baked Potato (Harry Starker's)   73
Tomate aux Concombres à la Crème (La Bonne Auberge)   34

DINING IN—THE GREAT CITIES

A Collection of Gourmet Recipes from the Finest Chefs in the Country

If you enjoyed *Dining In—Kansas City*, the following cookbook/restaurant guides are now available:

_____ Dining In—Baltimore	_____ Dining In—Pittsburgh
_____ Dining In—Boston	_____ Dining In—Portland
_____ Dining In—Chicago	_____ Dining In—St. Louis
_____ Dining In—Dallas	_____ Dining In—San Francisco
_____ Dining In—Honolulu/Maui	_____ Dining In—Seattle, Vol. II
_____ Dining In—Houston, Vol. I	_____ Dining In—Toronto
_____ Dining In—Houston, Vol. II	
_____ Dining In—Kansas City	
_____ Dining In—Los Angeles	
_____ Dining In—Minneapolis/St. Paul	_____ Feasting In—Atlanta
_____ Dining In—Monterey Peninsula	_____ Feasting In—New Orleans

Forthcoming:

_____ Dining In—San Diego

To order send $7.95 plus $1.00 postage and handling for each book.

CHECK HERE IF YOU WOULD LIKE TO HAVE A
☐ DIFFERENT *DINING IN—* COOKBOOK SENT TO YOU
ONCE A MONTH.

Payable by Mastercard, Visa or C.O.D. Returnable if not satisfied.
$7.95 plus $1.00 postage and handling for each book.

BILL TO: _____

Name _____

Address _____

City _____ State _____ Zip _____

☐ Payment enclosed   ☐ Send COD

☐ Charge

Visa # _____

Exp. Date _____

Mastercard # _____

Exp. Date _____

Signature _____

SHIP TO: _____

Name _____

Address _____

City _____ State _____ Zip _____

....

Name _____

Address _____

City _____ State _____ Zip _____

....

Name _____

Address _____

City _____ State _____ Zip _____

PEANUT BUTTER PUBLISHING

PEANUT BUTTER TOWERS · 2733 4TH AVENUE SOUTH · SEATTLE, WA 98134